THE BIZARRE WORLD OF EUROPEAN SPORTS

THE

BIZARRE

WORLD

OF

By Robert Daley

European
Sports

WILLIAM MORROW AND COMPANY

NEW YORK • 1963

For J R

Other Books by the Author

The World Beneath the City
Cars at Speed

Contents

VII

Contents

Photo Stories

THE BIZARRE WORLD OF EUROPEAN SPORTS

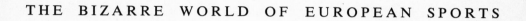

1

Exploit

THE WORLD OF EUROPEAN SPORT

ON its eighteenth day, when most of the men were already exhausted, the Tour de France bike race pedaled up and over Restefond Pass, nearly 9,300 feet high, the highest road in the Alps. That day's stage started at Antibes—sea level—and as soon as the road began to climb a Belgian named Eddy Pauwels sprinted out ahead of the pack.

Up and up hurried Pauwels, pedaling hard, and as he neared the pass he was minutes ahead of the pack. The race was above the clouds now, the air so fine a man could scarcely breathe, much less pedal a bike. As Pauwels crossed the pass, sweat was streaming off him, he was gasping for breath and his eyes were glazed by fatigue.

Down into the valley he plunged, sometimes at speeds of sixty miles per hour or more, the frail bike shivering with strain as he wrenched it around turns; then up, up again, over other passes. He was still ahead, but so tired now he began to crash. Three times in simple bends he was thrown to the road. Also, the road tore his tires to bits. He got five flats, fixing them himself, frantically, his fingers fumbling with valves, pumps, spokes, half-crazed with haste and exhaustion. Each time he remounted, wiped the blood from his face, and pedaled on.

The flats and the crashes took all that was left out of Eddy Pauwels. After leading the race over the highest part of the Alps, he was caught up and passed by the pack in the final few miles before the night's finish line. For nearly nine hours he had led the race; in the end he got nothing.

Except that he was the hero of all Europe, loved for "attacking" Restefond Pass, loved for the flats, loved for the crashes, loved for the way he sobbed so bitterly at the finish. Newspaper stories called him "valiant," as "magnificent" as the mountains themselves. TV cameras closed up on him; "What I have done, no beast would have done," he said, and the tears rolled down, streaking the sweat, dust, and blood on his face. Europe wanted to hold him in her arms.

Literally and emotionally, that day was the high point of the 1962 Tour de France, and also of sports in Europe for the year. It was a day of terrible effort, of suffering and pain, of raw danger, of man tiny and lost amid the towering mountains, yet conquering them with his heart and his will. It was a day of grandeur.

For what is really admired in sports in Europe is individual exploit: one man against some sort of terrible adversary. This does not mean another man. To be really exciting to a European the adversary should be partly brute nature at its most fearsome: the sheer wall of a mountain, the sea, a wild beast, tremendous distance, the speed of a race car hurtling past walls and trees; and secondly, the adversary should be partly man himself, his weaknesses as a man: fear and fatigue.

There is violence in sport everywhere, even if only the limited violence of the home run; but in Europe it is a different kind of violence, and there is much more of it. There are reasons why this is so.

Firstly, there is more sport to begin with because there are so many countries so close together, all of them engaging in certain common sports such as car racing and soccer, but all guarding also sports out of their own past: bullfighting in Spain; bareknuckle boxing bouts still fought clandestinely in

2

Britain; bareback horse races round the cobblestone piazzas of Italian towns.

And secondly, there is more violence because Europe is a continent of still smoldering passions; yet it is an orderly place too. If there were little order (as in Black Africa and parts of Asia and South America) there would be little sport or none at all. And if the people of Europe were as friendly and secure as most Americans, there would be less violence. But the people of Europe are not friendly and secure. On the whole they are suspicious. They keep expecting something to erupt. They have lived with violence a long time. They are used to it.

And so they find violence in their sport—or put it there. With one exception, games do not really interest them. Too tame. The exception is soccer, a diversion akin to baseball in that there is no violence, no body contact at all, in either game when properly played.

That is, in soccer there is no violence on the playing field. There is often plenty, too much, even, in the grandstand. Three or four times a year in countries as widely different in temperament as Poland, Italy, Austria, and Spain fans go berserk at soccer matches. Players have been shot from the grandstand, or kayoed by rocks, although this is less usual than general riots. Some riots are colossal in size. In a towering rage fans tear out seats to fling at players and officials— and also at each other. The fixtures of entire stadiums have been uprooted, destroyed, and while the riots last, players barricaded themselves in dressing rooms in fear and trembling. One team in Italy keeps a chauffeur and car, engine running, under the grandstand, ready to hustle the referee out of town the instant a riot starts.

Soccer riots and "incidents" are front page news in Europe. Fans read of them avidly. It has always seemed to me that the possibility of a riot, or at least a good fist fight in the grandstand, is one of the appeals of soccer. Certainly soccer stars, while well-paid and well-known in all the countries, are not nearly so rich and famous as an ace bike racer, car racer,

3

bullfighter. And if soccer matches draw big crowds, it is partly because there are so many of them, and because they are so much cheaper and more accessible than the heroic, violent sports.

For Europeans cannot wholeheartedly admire team spirit, team play, or team victory. Only Britain is strong on the *team;* teamwork is taught in the schools there during daily recreation periods, and many team games flourish. But for centuries in schools on the Continent boys have been given all work and no play. School often started at 8:00 A.M. and lasted till five or later in the afternoon. No recreation was organized. Boys, being boys, found ways to play, nonetheless, but mostly this meant running, jumping, climbing, something a boy could do on his own, or at least without any need for special equipment, special play areas or adult referees. Teams rarely existed, and boys learned nothing about teamwork. It was every man for himself. This became the national attitude, and carried over into national taste in sport. Sport must be individual, and if possible, terribly challenging.

Put a man, or two men roped together, on the north face of the Eiger Mountain in a storm, and Europe will wait anxiously to know what happens to them. If they are killed, no one will say, "They were asking for it." Instead the whole continent will be saddened, and the feeling will be that man (not just those two men) has been defeated again.

Recently a man named José Meiffret, aged fifty, pedaled a bicycle behind a Mercedes acting as windbreak at 128 miles per hour. This is insanely dangerous, of course. The record Meiffret broke was his own, for no one else is crazy enough to try such pedaling. There was no prize, monetary or otherwise, to be won. He did it because, he said, he was sure he could do it; therefore he had to.

The attempt, which took place on an autobahn in Germany, cost Meiffret, a Frenchman, about one thousand dollars. There is small chance he will get any of this back. All he has earned is fame, via television and newsreels, and the sympathy and admiration of nearly all Europeans.

4

Or take the case of Louis Lourmais, a swimmer who stroked his way fifty-three miles from Sein Island off the coast of Brittany, up the estuary of the Odet River to Quimper. There is no comprehensible reason why anyone should want to swim this route; it is not even a straight line. But Lourmais wanted to badly enough to stay in the water for three days. When finally he dragged himself onto the quai at Quimper an excited crowd applauded tumultuously. Lourmais could not have been too thrilled by this as he was trembling uncontrollably from fatigue, and could not even talk.

All over Europe individuals, on their own, constantly attempt feats which are bizarre, incredibly difficult and completely without significance. A fifty-six-year-old English lady hikes from the Scottish border to Land's End in twenty-three days. A Frenchman drives his motor scooter virtually nonstop from Rheims to Jerusalem and back during fifteen straight days.

Each time Europe watches avidly. Indeed, it is certainly the interest of the Continent, the receptions, flowers, speeches at the end which perpetuate such attempts at "exploits."

Most likely, America would be amused by some of these people, though not by many. All would be considered some kind of nut. The fifty-six-year-old English lady, Dr. Barbara Moore, hiking from Scotland south, drew such crowds that they trod on her feet; she held the front pages of Europe for weeks. Later, expecting a similar triumph, she marched from San Francisco to New York—to the massive indifference of the United States. This confused the old girl mightily, for her much shorter hike in Britain had made her the heroine of eighteen countries. When she got home, she began tramping about making petulant speeches, avowing her complete distaste for the New World.

On the organized level, sport in Europe still leans heavily on the individual, and on exploit. Europe is not so much interested in watching skill as in watching heroes cope with epic suffering, epic danger, epic fatigue.

The bike race is all of these things. The bike race came

into prominence in an era when everyone pedaled to work. Today the bicycle as transportation is ceasing to exist in Western Europe. Each year more cars and fewer bikes are sold, and hardly anyone rides bikes except the very young. Nonetheless, bike racing remains the queen of European sport, precisely because it satisfies all that a European demands of sport: it is individual, it is heroic in concept, grandiose in scale. Just to finish one is an exploit, meaning that at every finish line the fan has fifty or seventy or a hundred heroes to applaud.

The twenty-two-day, 2,600-mile Tour de France bike race is world famous. But there are dozens of other Tours nearly as long: the Tour of Italy, Tour of Spain, Tour of Yugoslavia, Tour of Switzerland, Tour of Luxembourg, and so on. The Communists run a Tour from East Berlin to Prague to Warsaw, but call it the Peace Race.

Bike races last so long, involve so many racers (sometimes more than a hundred fifty start a major Tour) and spend so many days high in the mountains that drama, violence—in short, *exploit*—are virtually inevitable.

Consider the most recent Tour of Italy. Three weeks in length, it was to pedal over Alps, Apennines and Dolomites for twelve days; often the route would be dirt roads high up and soaked by spring thaws.

For two weeks nothing much happened, beyond a few crashes, a few fights, a few accusations of collusion, doping and the like. There was no blistering heat on the plain, and the mountains were high but docile enough. Then, in the Dolomites, a blizzard struck the race.

For seven hours the race pedaled up through wind and storm. Snow fell steadily. It was bitterly cold. Shivering riders begged sweaters, pants, gloves from coaches, officials, and journalists following in cars. There were not enough to go round. Hour after hour the storm beat down on the race, the thin wheels running ever deeper, ever more slowly in the snow.

Riders abandoned by the dozens. The world champion, Rik

Van Looy, led twenty men into a farmhouse, where they huddled around a fire drinking all the wine and grapa they could find. The great Charly Gaul of Luxembourg stumbled up the mountain on foot, two Italian peasants trying to talk to him. One pushed Charly's bike, the other held an umbrella over his head.

Riders were taken away suffering from frostbitten fingers and toes. Peasants walked up and down the road collecting abandoned bikes. In all, fifty-five men abandoned the race during that one hallucinating stage, refusing to pedal anymore under the driving blizzard.

Europeans, reading about this the next day, were moved, excited, thrilled. To them, this was sport. This was the kind of emotion which no game, played according to rules under perfect conditions in some stadium somewhere, could ever give.

The prosaic sports do exist. There are international competitions every year in soccer, rugby, basketball, volley ball, water polo . . .

But in none of these sports does a man really risk anything. Not only do men not risk their lives, they do not even risk defeat or glory, both of which accrue only to the team. The European wants to cheer (or revile) a man like himself, one man, not a mass, not a team. And so some Europeans are interested in one or more team sports, but Europe as a whole is not.

To draw any kind of crowd for such events, it must seem nation against nation, rather than team against team. Let flags wave and anthems play, and Europe then will watch. If it cannot be man against exploit, then let it be one nation's team (youth) against another nation's team (youth), and all can watch and cheer in a spirit of patriotism. This is true even in soccer, where the biggest matches by far are international matches, and where there are now about thirty major international tournaments per year.

I do not mean to give the impression that Europe as a whole is bloodthirsty. I do not think it is. Few, if any, Europeans attend the blood sports (so-called) hoping to see blood. They have seen enough of that in their own towns, on their own doorsteps in other years. No, the audience is there to watch man cope. Cope with the brute enemy, with his own nerves, with fatigue. Cope with being a man.

Europe does not admire daredevils. The car racer is a big man in Europe, but this is because the European sees him as an individual trying to make a living in the most dangerous of all sports; if he were truly a daredevil (the European feels) he would have been dead long ago. Ski racers are considered much more foolhardy and are much less highly regarded. The skier is known to be a very young man probably of peasant stock who is stronger in the legs than the head. However, the skier is credited with great skill, because merely to get to the bottom in one piece is an achievement. The tracks in Europe (man against the mountain again) are bulldozed sheer and treeless so that the skiers often exceed sixty miles per hour standing on their own two feet. On one track in Italy, Adrien Duvillard of France averaged fifty-nine miles per hour winning, and at the steepest part of the track was clocked at eighty-three.

The European is fascinated by speed, understanding the lure; and by weight lifting too, understanding that under the ponderous load thick-thighed man is at his most frail, for his tendency to overreach himself is ultimately irresistible.

Most of all, the European is fascinated by suffering, especially if it is colossal enough; most years in the spring there is a walking race, 285 miles from Strasbourg to Paris, nonstop, during three days and nights, up and over the "wall of sleep" that third night into Paris while Europe watches baffled, yet full of wonder: how can men do it? Each summer hordes of people swim, or fail to swim, the English Channel; in the East they are hauled shivering and exhausted out of the Bosporus and the Caspian Sea just about as often. There used to be a three-day bike race nonstop (Paris-Brest-Paris) and there still is one which lasts about sixteen hours, leaving Bordeaux at two o'clock in the morning and reaching Paris late the next afternoon. There is an eight-day car race (the Auto Tour of France) which is contested virtually nonstop, the men finishing dirty, unshaven, and half-blind with the need to sleep. In the Alps nearly every expedition lasts two days or more. Once an Italian, Walter Bonatti, scaled the Aiguille du Dru alone. It took him seven days. For most of six nights he slept standing up in a sleeping bag hanging by a rope over the black void. Each day he inched a little higher. The skin was gone from his hands, he was numb with cold, tortured by thirst. Terror and exhaustion fought for control of his soul. On the seventh day he clawed his way over the peak—and was joyously pummeled and embraced by a group of his friends, who had come up the "easy" way.

Skill and competition are admired by the European. But it is exploit that he loves.

2

Confusion and Emotion

THE WORLD OF THE OLYMPICS

THERE is little nationalism in American sport. I would like to believe we are above the kind of chauvinistic fervor which so often spoils sport in Europe. But perhaps we are not. Perhaps it is just that we rarely play anything internationally and consequently are not reduced to impotent rage at the foreign teams that are trouncing us.

For American athletes there is only one international competition that counts: the Olympics. Every four years we expect to win the most gold medals in track and field because we have the best runners and jumpers. We expect to do even better in swimming, and we discount all other twenty Olympic sports as being unimportant.

The Olympics for America is sport, purely and simply. In Europe the Olympics is something else. Each European nation staging the Games must, simply must, stage a more gorgeous spectacle than has ever been staged before. It also must, simply must, win a tremendous number of gold medals.

Anything else is national disgrace.

Each other European nation must, simply must, win gold medals in proportion to its size. If it doesn't, there will be heated speeches back home and investigations in the national

10

assembly; fist fights may even break out among the deputies.

In 1960 Italy tried so hard to outdo all previous Olympic Games in gorgeousness that the effect, at times, was farcical. Italy also tried so hard to win gold medals (and succeeded) that it was accused of cheating by other European teams. It seems that the Italian soccer, boxing, and cycling federations had been holding back amateurs for three years; no young amateur was allowed to turn pro until after the Games. Thus Italy won all but one Olympic bike race, and had men in six of the ten boxing finals.

France, meanwhile, won no gold medals at all in anything. A period of national shame followed the Games. Sports officials were sacked and a new budget voted. In 1959, preparing for the '60 games, France's Olympic budget was 1,650,000 francs; for 1963 it is 7,421,000 francs. France expects to do better at Tokyo in 1964 than it did at Rome.

So each Olympic Games tournament is sport, but it is never purely sport, at least not for Europe. During an Olympic meet, the various committees and officials are under even more pressure than the athletes. They, too, must break world's records. They, too, must strive for perfection.

They, too, choke up in the clutch. If Olympic gold shines through anyway, it is despite them.

I   Confusion

Pageantry, excitement, crowds, competition — all Olympics have. The one at Rome also had empty hotel rooms, empty seats and surplus confusion. Confusion is something of an Italian birthright, and was to be expected whether a million tourists came or a dozen.

For instance, at the opening ceremony there were no tickets to be bought, but the stadium never did fill completely. There were patches of empty seats in several places.

Where were the missing tickets? In a drawer somewhere?

A few hours before the ceremony the Mexican delegation had spent hours pleading with Olympic officials for the right to buy twenty tickets. The Mexicans had paid for these tickets months before. They had receipts. But their tickets had been given to someone else—no one knew whom.

The Italian officials were profusely sorry about this. The Mexicans begged to be allowed to pay for the tickets a second time. Just give them the tickets.

Each Italian Olympic official in turn had no tickets, but was extremely gracious, extremely sympathetic. Italians are always gracious, always sympathetic. Even the Mexicans weren't able to stay mad at them long.

The ticket situation was vague to the very end. The ticket chief, Dr. Fausto Cattani, said they had been so busy in his department they hadn't counted the money since July. He said he had no idea how many tickets had been sold.

The Olympic village was incredibly well-guarded. There was a high wire fence, patrolled by sabre-toting cops on horseback. Vladimir Kuts, a multiple Olympic champion in 1956, but only a tourist in 1960, could not get in until the head of the Soviet delegation personally went out and approved Kuts's entry. One competitor, the Australian Noel Freeman, was strolling through the village one day. Detectives arrested him, dragged him to the gate, and threw him out. They said his identity papers were not in order.

From an elevated road which passed over part of the village, hundreds of people leaned over the parapet each day watching the athletes and detectives. It was like persons staring down into a zoo, wondering what keepers and beasts might do next.

All the stadiums, particularly the two Sports Palaces designed by Pier Nervi, were both beautiful and functional, but one had to pass through several concentric steel fences to get to them, surrendering stubs to ticket takers at each fence. The first fence was usually a hundred yards outside the stadium. Tickets were good at one gate only, and if you turned up at the wrong gate you had to walk around the outside steel fence to get to the proper one. This added a mile or so hike to the daily entertainment of most spectators.

The stadiums all swarmed with ushers, most of whom gave the impression of never having been in the stadium before. There were so many numbers on each ticket that no man could have found his seat unaided.

Consequently, several ushers had a conference before deciding that your seat actually was on the other side of the stadium.

Outside the stadiums none of the police knew where the parking lots were. But all were willing to discuss the problem with you—advising you to watch out for a certain one-way street because if you got on it, it would be six kilometers before you could turn around.

Mostly, the confusion, the empty seats, the empty hotel rooms, the furious patrons were due to too many officials, ticket takers, and policemen. There were thousands of them. As one Roman put it, "We did a magnificent job of preparation, but once everything was ready we should have called in twenty Germans to handle it from there."

II Emotion

The opening of any Olympics is a heart-stirring spectacle. One can suppose he will watch unmoved. It is not possible.

There is too much there as the teams parade in—and not just color and martial music. There is ancient and modern history, there is tragedy, there is weakness, there is strength. There is as much politics, both overt and symbolic, as in most elections.

Greece leads the parade. This is fitting because it formed Western civilization. But it is no longer a significant competitor and its band is small.

The Afghanistan team wears charcoal-gray slacks and white jackets and marches swinging arms high. The blue-suited Belgians wear white gloves; the Bermudians, of course, Bermuda shorts.

The Bulgarians wave miniature Bulgarian flags at the

crowd. They are led by four girls in jonquil frocks. The men wear green. Two tieless, burly men in baggy gray suits bring up the rear. Are they gate crashers, or what?

The Canadians are the only team to march in shirt sleeves. The girls wear white suits with red handbags and red trim.

There are eleven Chileans, one of them a girl who carries her nation's flag. This delegation was to have numbered about eighty. Then earthquakes racked the entire country. There was no money for an Olympic team. The nations of Europe chipped in enough to bring those athletes who still wanted to compete. To see the Chileans there warms the heart. This is what sport is all about.

The Danes wear red jackets and white slacks.

Two of the five Fiji Islanders wear a male version of the sarong.

Taiwan (Formosa) passes in parade and its leader whips out a hand-painted banner: Under Protest. The team had entered under the name of Nationalist China. The International Olympic Committee was the first world body to say it no longer represented China and to march as Formosa or go home.

The French march by wearing berets—the men blue ones, the girls white.

The two Germanys march together under a special Olympic flag. The I.O.C. has arranged that, too.

Haiti's team is two men. One carries the flag, the other marches behind.

The Indians wear blue slacks, white jackets, and brilliant gold-colored turbans.

The Irish wear green, naturally. Ron Delany, the defending champion in the 1,500-meter run, carries the flag.

The Kenya uniform is as mixed as the races that compose the nation. Some of the men are white, some Negro, some Indian; and they wear turbans, Panama hats or no hat at all, as they choose. But they all march in step.

The Liberians parade by under gold fezzes. Mal Whitfield, an American, a two-time Olympic champion and their coach, proudly brings up the rear. Who says a man cannot represent two countries with honor?

The Pakistan team wears white turbans with huge flowing topknots.

The Poles are in aquamarine jackets and greenish baize pants.

The Rumanians wear deep amber jackets and wave flags at the crowd.

The United States goes by. The shivers run up and down a man's spine and there is a mist of pride in his eyes. Rafer Johnson, a Negro, carries his country's flag, cradling it as if it were a baby or something fragile that he must not drop. He walks very tall and proud.

The Russians are the biggest group. Their leader holds the flag at arm's length in one hand, the pole exactly perpendicular, the flag flowing back over his head. It takes perhaps ten minutes to circle the track, and one waits for the man's arm to collapse from the strain. But he never flinches, and when his delegation is finally all in place he is still holding the flag out there in one hand at arm's length.

Then the Italians enter and a mighty cheer goes up. The parade ends. Bombs burst behind the stadium. At the edge of the field five thousand pigeons are released.

The pigeons flutter in the bowl of the stadium as densely as confetti and paper in a ticker-tape parade. A swarm of locusts must look like that.

The sky for a moment is gray, then the birds fly off—all of them at once. All the bells of Rome begin ringing. The tolling goes on and on.

Speeches are made, and a boy runs in with the Olympic torch. He laps the track, then runs up the steps toward the bronze saucer of the rim of the stadium. It is a long, very steep run. One imagines he must be gasping for breath, and never mind the glory of the moment.

After two hours the ceremony ends. The teams march out. One watches the flags pass again. One is amazed at how many variations of the British flag there are, how many colonies

15

there once had been, how many brand-new nations now.

The Moslem teams, from India to Egypt, have no women athletes. Their women are home wearing veils.

One marvels at the colors of the uniforms, the crowd, the stadium, the sunny Roman afternoon.

One thinks of how much color there is in the world, how much of the story of man parades before one's eyes each time the Olympics open.

III Confusion Again

Several Olympic events did not get much publicity in American newspapers and this is too bad as they were among the most interesting. Such events were called: the program-hunting contest; the four-mile walk around the stadium from the parking lot; the 200-yard obstacle race through various gates and ticket checkers to the press box; entering the Olympic village.

Entries in all these events were restricted to newsmen covering the Olympics. The object of each was to outwit the Italians. Any contestant who lost his temper or started cursing was disqualified.

The program-hunting contest was one of the most interesting events. Free programs were distributed to all reporters each morning at the press center five miles outside of Rome (about an hour, round trip by cab through traffic). To devote an hour to this single event meant to risk losing the various other events later in the day and so most of us preferred to arrive at the stadium without programs. We hoped to be able to pick one up during the four-mile walk event, around the stadium from the press parking lot. No programs were distributed or sold in or near the press box, naturally, as this would not have been sporting.

Most of the reporters never got over the surprise of being able to arrive at the stadium without having seen a program seller. Many program sellers were reputed to be hidden near by, but it was difficult to find them as they were working just

16

as hard to outwit prospective buyers, as buyers were working to outwit them.

Booths selling tickets also were hidden near the stadium. On the ninth day I accidentally found them. I had spied a program seller, who started running, of course. I ran after him, and was gaining slightly when suddenly in a clump of trees, I spied the booths. They were 400 yards from the gates, hidden partly by the trees, partly by the swimming pool. There were no customers. I saw that I was the first to find them, and the thrill of it welled up inside me. I was so moved that I stood gazing at them in awe, and the program seller got away.

Anyhow, after the program hunt, and the four-mile walk from the press parking lot, came the big event of each day— the 200-yard obstacle race from the first preliminary gate to the press box.

A pass, a badge, and at least one ticket were required for the race. At the first fence there were about twenty gates, all funneling into one runway. Naturally the pass and badge were honored only at one of the twenty gates, and naturally it was the one at the extreme left, about thirty yards farther on. But what is thirty yards after that four-mile hike from the parking lot?

After passing this first gate, many contestants seemed to feel they had won, and they put their passes and credentials in carefully buttoned inside pockets for safety. This was definitely a mistake.

All credentials had to be presented at least twice more, once when passing inside the stadium wall, once at the top of the stairs, and usually once to the usher. At least one of these checkers punched one of your passes, and contestants won or lost points depending upon how gracefully they could hand it over while carrying a briefcase, typewriter, binoculars, and holding the passport-type pass in the other hand with the photo showing.

Each time you left to file copy or to go to the men's room, part of this process was repeated. And if you ever went outside of the stadium entirely, you could not get back in until

17

tomorrow. Naturally many contestants lost points over this rule, and some of them, finding that they could not re-enter the press box after descending to try to interview athletes, actually got angry and were disqualified completely.

The track stadium was easier to enter than the swimming stadium, because the swimming was at night and it was difficult for each checker to peer at the photo on your pass and tell if it was really you. So entering the swimming stadium took a little time. It was another place where many contestants began to splutter and lost valuable points.

The event called "entering the Olympic village" was one which required gamesmanship of the highest order. If you wanted to interview athletes or coaches, the normal procedure was to turn in all credentials at the gate, sign some papers, and post a bond of $1,000 that you would not talk to anyone while you were in there. But this took time, and you either had to be out again before 12:30 or stay till 2:00. In other words, it was a pretty big risk.

The *Paris Match* magazine people solved this problem by hiring a Coca-Cola truck and Coca-Cola uniforms. Then they would drive up to the gate honking like mad. Naturally the gatekeeper never hesitated. Coca-Cola must go through. Any man who says different is subversive, even in Italy. The gatekeeper would fling open the gates, snap to attention and salute as the truck roared through, the *Paris Match* boys laughing like madmen.

But *The New York Times* could never stoop to this. Finally we decided to remove all press insignia, wear short pants and baseball caps with American flags on them, carry athletic-looking satchels instead of briefcases, and start running toward the gate from a hundred yards away, as if we were milers dashing back from a spirited workout at the practice field. This tactic never failed. Occasionally we varied it by tying handkerchiefs around our necks and coming in heel-and-toe like the 20,000-meter walkers.

There were many other lesser events too, such as the very popular "leaving the stadium after filing." The object of this was to guess which unlighted gate the Italians had left open, and then to find it in the dark without having to circle the stadium more than twice. This was very popular with some men, but others were too tired and decided simply to spend the night in the press box, which, of course, gave them a very big lead in the next day's events.

Actually I was disqualified for bitterness the second day, but many reporters kept smiling till the bitter end, and were awarded gold medals. These men usually had never had any experience with the Italians before, and actually thought all this was *funny*.

IV More Emotion

At the age of eighteen, Herb Elliott had given up running, liked to smoke, drink beer, keep late hours, and tool around Perth, Australia, on his motor scooter.

At twenty, he was the greatest and most dedicated running machine the world had ever seen. He smashed the 4-minute-mile barrier a dozen times, lowering the record finally to an incredible 3 minutes 54.5 seconds.

Then he got married, became a father, considered turning pro. He gave up the Spartan life, raced rarely, spoke lightly of his future. He said, in effect, "Having raced so fast once, I no longer have to train hard."

At twenty-two, he came to Rome for the Olympics, winner of half a dozen unimpressive races that season. He was relaxed and airy about his running now. He was, naturally, a potential winner of the 1,500-meter race. But his days as a record-breaker seemed over.

And then he won the 1,500 by thirty yards in 3:35.6. He ran faster than ever before in his life. He ran the equivalent of a 3:52.6 mile. He ran every other man into the ground. He destroyed the race. There was no race. There was simply Elliott, running on and on. Faster and faster. The others wilted, the gap behind him widened. He seemed all alone on the track. On and on. Faster, faster.

19

He was born in Perth on the twenty-fifth of February, 1938. His father had a home-furnishings business, but had been a top cross-country cyclist and loved all sports. As a child, Herb was, says his mother, always commanding and terribly aggressive. The boy went to a Catholic high school, got good marks in mathematics and ran the mile in 4:20.4.

Then he dropped a piano on his foot, crushing the foot. He was seventeen, gave up track for good and took up what he calls carousing.

But when the 1956 Olympics came to Melbourne, the Elliott family flew up from Perth. Herb watched enthralled—not at the 1,500-meter winner, Ron Delany, but at the Soviet, Vladimir Kuts, who won both the 5,000- and 10,000-meter runs.

It seemed to the eighteen-year-old Elliott that Kuts knew how to suffer, and suffering appealed to him.

He wrote to the mile record-holder, John Landy, for advice. Landy answered, encouraging him. And he met Percy Cerutty, a sixty-three-year-old physical fitness and diet fanatic.

Cerutty gave Elliott a body-building program which, some days, started with a breakfast of dry rolled oats, continued through swimming, weight lifting, a thirty-three-mile run in under four hours, and racing up an eight-story-high, sixty-degree sand dune forty-five times. Many days ended only when Elliott finally dropped from exhaustion.

After six weeks under Cerutty's domination, Elliott ran the mile in 4:06, or fourteen seconds faster than he had ever run before.

He moved to Melbourne to be near Percy, took a job there, and continued with the program until he was breaking four minutes for the mile every time he raced.

"You must learn to thrust against pain, and be contemptuous of it," Cerutty had told him.

"Once you start running," Elliott said, "you get a sensation of strain. The pain is something real. Sometimes, it hurts so much you're dying to stop. Your muscles are screaming,

20

but you keep going. It's a matter of will power. It's you that you've got to hurt."

And another time, he said: "You get bloody sick of training, but that's the time when you stick to it. That's when one runner proves himself better than the others. Anyone can do well when he's enthusiastic. It's when you stick to it that you show you're the superior man. Speed is a gift, but endurance is an achievement."

But once he had got married, Elliott seldom talked this way. He quit Cerutty, rarely raced, did not seem to train hard any more. Cerutty bawled him out publicly: Elliott has been hypnotized by his marriage, has lost the will to win. He must wake up, get rid of his present lethargic approach.

Elliott answered with an airy wave of his hand. "I have a backlog of strength from the years with Cerutty," he said.

He talked about the book he was writing on "personalities." He talked of his wife and son. He was relaxed when reporters spoke to him, no longer the testy youngster he had been.

He liked listening to classical music and read poetry. "Poetry," he said, "can make you a better man by giving you an appreciation of beauty and an awareness of things around you. It seems today that you've got to be an intellectual to be able to get back to nature."

He could not abide fools and "people who try to exploit me." He worried about his personality, and once wondered aloud whether too much physical exercise and living like an animal might stunt his intellect, slow down his mental advancement.

His critics felt such musings would slow down his running, prevent him from winning the Olympic 1,500-meter run. They were wrong.

The 1960 Olympics had much which sparkled: crossbow shooting in the Circus Maximus, while fluted trumpets blared; turbaned Sikhs slashing at the ball and each other's bare feet indiscriminately in the field hockey final; America's big, broad-shouldered, unbeatable girl swimmers. It had flags, pageants, world records, mobs of people. But Herb Elliott

21

was the high point. Running on and on, faster and faster, he was youth, stamina, ruthless will. He dominated the race, himself, the stadium. He was the Olympic motto personified: Higher, Faster, Stronger. He was, for me at least, the noblest vision which amateur sport—sport for sport's sake—has to offer. I think I will see him running down the stretch, that enormous gap behind him, virtually alone on the track, faster, faster, straining toward the tape—I think I will remember that forever.

3

A Boy Shadowboxes the Past

THE WORLD OF MARCEL CERDAN, JR.

IF sport were pure, there would be no profit for anyone except the spiritual profit won by the competing athletes. There would be no organizers, promoters, coaches, managers. A boy would compete only because he wanted to and only for as long as it pleased him.

But sport is not pure, and often a boy is formed into an athlete by others for motives which have nothing to do with sport. Sometimes these motives have little enough to do with money; at times glory counts more than gold. It is hard for America, which has so many, many heroes in so many, many sports, to know what it is like to be German, Italian, French, and have so few.

One spring day in 1959 a fifteen-year-old boy weighing 132 pounds and standing about five feet five flew from Casablanca to Paris. The squad of reporters and photographers who met the plane were stunned by the sight of him.

"The same eyes," they murmured among themselves. "The same expressions, gestures, smile."

All agreed that the resemblance was stunning and that the future of boxing in France had never seemed so promising.

For the small, scared boy who got off the plane was Marcel Cerdan, Jr. He had come to Paris to learn to be a fighter like his father.

In France no hero lives as long nor shines as brightly as a dead hero. Marcel Cerdan had been dead ten years, killed in a plane crash thirteen months after winning the middleweight championship from Tony Zale, and four months after losing it to Jake La Motta.

As a man Cerdan was neither better nor worse than most men. As a boxer he was neither better nor worse than most champions. But he was killed at the summit of his life and so all France, given to revering dead heroes anyway, remembers him as a demigod. Not even Georges Carpentier, who is still alive, was as great a fighter, champion, or Frenchman as Marcel Cerdan.

"I put the gloves on for the first time almost a year ago," said the boy who got off the plane. He was very nervous. Flash bulbs popped, questions were fired at him. He did not know what to say.

In a few minutes he was whisked away to a gym to train. His manager was to be Philippe Filippi, the most prosperous manager in France. The boy would have his first fight the moment he was sixteen and legally eligible. He would win, of course. The arena would be packed. The boy would be stimulated to greatness by the greatness of the name he bore.

The door of the gym closed on Marcel Cerdan, Jr., and no further news came out of the place. Six months passed, then a television show was produced in honor of the tenth anniversary of the death of Cerdan, Sr.

The show opened with the camera focused on the back of a fighter punching the heavy bag in the gym.

The announcer's voice said: "This young man is—" There was a dramatic pause, then the fighter turned brusquely into the camera, which quickly closed up on his face—"Marcel Cerdan!"

A second camera was waiting in Casablanca, where the boy's mother said in an anguished voice: "I never wanted him to box. Boxing took my husband from me. I will know the same suffering with my son. I never saw my husband fight. I'll never go to see my son fight, either."

The announcer said to her softly: "Madame Cerdan, Marcel is in Paris watching you. On what you say to him now could depend his entire career. Speak to him"—the announcer paused as if to give the audience of millions a chance to swallow huskily—"speak to him from the heart."

In a small, humble voice Mme. Cerdan said: "It's cold in Paris, my little one. Be careful. Dress warmly."

The manager, Philippe Filippi, was asked to speak. He gazed into the camera and said piously: "I am a religious man and I know that Marcel up there is watching me and that he is happy about what I am doing for his boy."

In December, Marcel Cerdan, Jr., turned sixteen and applied for his license. Stories about him appeared in newspapers and magazines. Many of the illustrations showed him in a boxer's crouch with a great photo of his father staring down at him from the wall.

The boy lived with an uncle, Emile Lopez, in an apartment lent to them by a wealthy Parisien who had admired the boy's father. After breakfast of coffee and French bread sliced down the middle and toasted on one side, Marcel would go out to jog for an hour in the Bois de Boulogne, the Central Park of Paris.

In the evening the uncle would drive him to a dingy, one-room gym on the south side. Marcel would pound away at the heavy bag, then go two rounds in the ring with another boy, often getting his nose bloodied. He wore a headgear in the ring, but the tissue above his eyes was thickening. The months passed. He trained every day, absorbing hundreds of punches. The headgear could not stop them all.

Between morning and evening workouts, the boy's time was his own. He lay on his bed listening to his Elvis Presley records, or leafed through magazines and comic books or went to the movies. Sometimes he hung about the park hoping to

25

be invited to join the games of other boys his own age. Because he did not go to school, he knew no one except those he had met in the gym. School bored him, so he quit going. It was difficult to say who was responsible for that, or for his desire to be a fighter.

"I want to be a fighter because I love only that," the boy said.

"It was Marcel's idea," the uncle asserted. "I was down in Casablanca last year and saw him on the beach and I said to him, "Well, Marcel, what are you going to do with your life? Are you going to work all your life in the bar with your mother, or do you want to try boxing?"

At this time Philippe Filippi was in Casablanca with another boxer. Lopez arranged for him to watch Marcel work out. Filippi decided the boy had possibilities, and agreed to handle him. Lopez, despite the tears of his sister, Marinette Cerdan, then brought Marcel to Paris. Lopez took care of room and board. Mme. Cerdan sent pocket money.

Lopez had met the late Marcel Cerdan only once, but like most French boxing fans, believed he was the greatest middleweight of all time.

"He was the complete fighter," Lopez says earnestly. "Boxer, puncher—complete." His eyes shone as he spoke. He had never seen Marcel Cerdan fight.

Lopez was twenty-nine, unmarried, a pants-presser by trade. He was a sincere, likable young man who seemed to see in Marcel Cerdan's son a way to make both himself and the boy rich and famous. Lopez even provided the boy with a record album of English lessons so that he could fight in America and make a fortune. However, the boy was bored by them.

I received the impression that Marcel Cerdan, Jr., was the private dream of M. Lopez. Philippe Filippi would be there to collect, if the time came, but his investment was small. But Lopez seemed to have invested all his hope in the boy—who, after only a few months, was already out of his control.

26

When Lopez brought a journalist—myself—around, the boy refused to talk until he got permission from his trainer, a broken-nosed ex-pug named Marcel Petit. Lopez pleaded with the boy to be polite. The boy refused. Lopez apologized profusely after the boy had gone off.

That night in the gym Lopez hollered instructions as Marcel sparred. Suddenly the boy broke off the sparring, turned and told Lopez to shut up, he was not a trainer, did not know anything about boxing.

As Marcel trained, it was obvious that he would love to get in the ring and bash somebody. The heavy bag bored him. As he punched it, his eyes roved restlessly about the filthy little gym and he was soon winded and punching listlessly. He was solidly built. He had no stinging punch, and when someone hit him in the ring he got furious and forgot tactics in an effort to hit back.

He seemed a surly youth, or perhaps only bewildered. Local articles had him redeeming French boxing in a few years. He appeared to like this idea, and his eyes lit up when he talked about it.

Several more months passed. His first fight was postponed three times.

The first fight of Marcel Cerdan, Jr., drew a packed house —more than 2,000 fans—to Paris's tiny Salle Wagram. The place was filled with film stars and other celebrities, and several rows of seats normally sold had to be given over to the press and photographers.

Dozens of photographers mobbed the boy as he climbed into the ring. Their flashes blinded him and he looked scared as he waved to the crowd. The place rocked with cheers as his name was announced.

The other boy, also an amateur, was a North African named Ait Tayeb. He had had six fights already. His bathrobe, in contrast to Marcel's chic silk one, was shabby, and he had only his two or three handlers rooting for him in all that crowd.

The matchmaker, Gilbert Benaim, had signed Tayeb the

27

night before, after searching for weeks for an opponent "suitable" for young Cerdan. Neither Benaim nor Philippe Filippi wanted an opponent who might win the fight. Managers readying other young boxers wanted no part of Marcel, his build-up, and a crowd solidly behind him.

"Finding Tayeb," Benaim said, "was tougher than finding a main event fighter."

As the bell rang, Marcel Cerdan, Jr., looked paralyzed by stage fright. Then he moved forward, his head lolling from side to side. He was evidently too nervous to keep it still.

Some tentative punches were exchanged. The North African, equally scared, stung Marcel twice. Each time, Marcel seemed to lose his head, rushing forward to swing furious roundhouse rights which missed. During the last of the three two-minute rounds, Marcel's arms got so heavy with fatigue he could scarcely lift them to punch.

There was not much else to report. The final bell rang. An announcer climbed into the ring and cried into the microphone:

"The winner: Marcel Cerdan, Jr!"

The arena went wild with delight.

Newspaper dispatches the next day indicated that the fight was either inconclusive or a disaster, depending upon how much you had admired the boy's dad. Nearly all the reports spoke more of the great Marcel Cerdan than of this pale, scared boy who resembled him so much. They spoke of how Marcel had knocked out Zale, how he had lost only four of 111 fights, how he had begun in that same ring twenty-three years before. Perhaps Junior could learn; his dad had been such a glory to boxing and to France.

There were a couple of more fights in Paris. Bad publicity mounted and it was clear that soon no gloss would be left on the name of Marcel Cerdan. Philippe Filippi took the boy into the provinces, where he fought regularly at places like Maubeuge, Coutances, Nogent, Vertgalant. His opponents were mostly North Africans, all hand-picked by Filippi. Cerdan suffered one draw. He won every other fight, more than twenty as this is written. There were no write-ups in Paris, few boxing experts bothered to go so far to see for themselves, and Filippi, when questioned, was reticent. Cerdan had knocked no one out, but had scored two TKO's. One of his hand-picked opponents proved so small as to be rejected by the boxing board as soon as he had got off the scale.

More than three years have passed since the first fight of Marcel Cerdan, Jr. He is still boxing regularly in the provinces, his brows thickening, his nose flatter. Sometimes you can find his name in the results of weekend bouts which the Paris papers publish every Monday morning. Filippi, questioned, will remark halfheartedly that the boy is going to hurt a lot of fighters someday. But he hasn't yet, and few people now believe what was widely believed at first—that he will soon redeem the low state of French pugilism. No one talks about his father much at all.

4

How To Tell Good from Evil

THE WORLD OF
FRENCH WRESTLING

To remove all gloom, it must be admitted that wrestling exists in Europe too. . . .

Of course, even wrestling takes advantage of supposed nationalistic traits. Thus all Orientals become Japanese, wear foot-long mustaches and practice mysterious holds and moves that the crowd does not understand but believes to be judo. Men billed as Germans have screamed "Heil Hitler!" at the crowd; this establishes them as villains. A wrestler from Israel is always known as Rabbi somebody, and one from Budapest is called "The Butcher." Are not all Central Europeans (particularly wrestlers) but one step removed from barbarism?

As every wrestling fan knows, Scotsmen are terrible tightwads, wear kilts over their trunks, and enter the ring to the strains of a bagpipe. The number one Scottish wrestler right now is Jamie MacTiffen. When Jamie is winning, supporters of the other man start raining coins upon the ring. Jamie, remember, is a Scot, and Scotsmen are terrible tightwads, according to the script. The crowd can watch Jamie eyeing the money, watch his expression change and his hold loosen as avarice gets the better of him.

30

Finally, Jamie lets go of his man and dives for the money. He is still reaching for it as the other wrestler pins him, winning the match. The bagpipes play a lament as the beaten Jamie stumbles back to his dressing room.

All Gaul is divided into two parts, the one led by Robert Lageat, the other by Alex Goldstein. These are the two Caesars of French and—by extension—European wrestling. Lageat has Spartacus, the Hangman, and Kamikaze-the-suicidal-Jap. Goldstein has Zorro, the Masked Man, and Beautiful Bobby Duranton.

Lageat and Goldstein are locked in a death struggle. Goldstein has his fingers clamped on Lageat's throat and is slowly strangling him. In all of French wrestling, the two promoters' faces are almost the only ones you can see. The wrestlers are all masked or perfumed or midgets—or all three. Goldstein is small, well-dressed, shrewd, a business man. Lageat is an ex-wrestler. Goldstein has put slapstick comedy into his shows. He paints with broad strokes, making the audience laugh with pies in the face. Lageat hates Goldstein, accuses him of deforming wrestling. Lageat sees wrestling as discipline and truth. "There is nothing more beautiful than wrestling," he says earnestly.

Goldstein is killing him with laughter. Lageat, the ex-wrestler, cannot see this. Every time Goldstein hurls him (figuratively) out of the ring, Lageat plods doggedly back for more. Goldstein's business is booming; Lageat's receipts drop every week. Lageat cannot work out what is happening to him.

Goldstein is fifty-three. He began promoting wrestling as France was liberated. For fourteen years he made a living, not much more. On December 8, 1958, he launched the Masked Man (six feet three, 260 pounds, dressed all in black except for studded leather belt in satanic red). A few days later the White Angel climbed into one of Goldstein's rings. The White Angel—white mask and white satin cape—was 220 pounds of deeply tanned, beautifully muscled man. His heart was pure; the Masked Man's heart is as foul as a sewer. After several months of build-up, Goldstein matched the two of them before the biggest gate of his career. Goldstein needed no further urging. More and more masked grapplers joined his stable, as did freaks of all kinds including the midgets Bruno Ledez ("The Miniature Apollo") and Stani Kovalic, known as "The Polish Assassin"—all forty inches of him. The money poured in. The popularity of wrestling expanded in Paris and spread all over Western Europe. There were the Masked Judge, the Phantom, Superman and a Vampire whose specialty was sucking blood from opponents' throats—if the Vamp once got his fangs into you, you were done.

There are now seven wrestling arenas in Paris, a dozen more in the suburbs, and in a good week, a fan could easily see two shows a day, every day. There are other promoters besides Goldstein and Lageat who share or shared in all this loot, but Goldstein and Lageat with their associates are the biggest ones, and control the most European rings and wrestlers.

Goldstein did not invent masked wrestlers; he claims that the Angel and the others came to him ready-masked, and even they were not the first. Goldstein did not invent the perfumed, pretended homosexual wrestler; Gorgeous George existed long before Goldstein's Bobby Duranton. Goldstein was not the first to equip a wrestler with a valet or butler, either, nor was he the first at whose shows fans rioted.

But no promoter before him ever packed an evening with so much comedy, so much slapstick, pantomime, so much rioting by fans, so much laughter and incipient tragedy all at once. At its best, Goldstein's art and timing are on a Mack Sennett level. Goldstein will not admit to stage-managing his bouts, but it is impossible to believe that his wrestlers think up the gags themselves. His shows are too perfect, too all of a piece.

The first bout may feature ordinary wrestlers, one of whom has an Oriental cast to his features. According to the card, the other is a German; Goldstein has named him "Dr. Adolf

Kaiser." One can almost see Goldstein puzzling over an adequate Teutonic name, reluctantly discarding Adolf Hitler, and then Kaiser Wilhelm, as not being subtle enough. The choice came down to either Adolf Kaiser or Wilhelm Hitler. Goldstein will tell you with an almost straight face that he is a man of good taste, and not a stage-manager at all.

Anyway, Dr. Adolf Kaiser is equipped with a heel-clicking, German-General-Staff-type bow, and the Oriental has an Oriental-type bow. Every time one slugs the other, all through the bout, they step back and bow. It is quietly, vastly amusing, and sets the tone.

In bout number two, Bobby Duranton is matched against someone; it does not matter whom. Bobby's bleached blond curls hang to his shoulders, his fingernails are painted, he wears a brocaded dressing gown, and is attended by his valet, Firmin. Bobby, doing the nancy-boy act while ministered to by the solicitous Firmin, is funny. Bobby getting beaten up by the other wrestler is funny, too. The distraught Firmin, trying to leap to his master's aid though restrained by police and officials, is also funny. When Firmin breaks loose, kayoes the other wrestler and raises the groggy Bobby's arm in victory, half the crowd screams "Foul!" "Dirty brute!" and worse, while sophisticated fans laugh till the tears come. The referee disqualifies Bobby. The valet knocks the ref cold and raises Bobby's arm again. The referee, held up by two policemen, screams chokingly into the mike that Duranton is disqualified. The valet starts toward the ref again. Bobby grasps the valet, but it does no good. The solution would be to fire the bum.

Bout number three surely would feature the "irascible" Masked Man. The Masked Man is so mean that the crowd is still mad at him from the last time he appeared. He shakes his fist at the mob to show he doesn't care. He spits at them, and when the bout starts he fouls his opponent liberally and with great skill.

Fruit begins to shower down from the high seats. A group of young toughs rush the ring. A line of cops cuts them off, wrestles with them. The fruit is still raining down. A tomato always catches one cop flush in the puss. The Masked Man always leaps out of the ring to slug one of the toughs, and he usually spits on somebody's wife.

Some of this and other riots obviously are part of the show: surely stooges threw the first tomatoes and led the charge on the ring. But how much is staged? And where did Goldstein get that dead-eye who can hit a cop in the face with a tomato every time?

The slapstick comedy in these riots is funny, staged or not. One can not fail to laugh when the tomato hits the cop. The second or third time you see it, it's still funny.

But the entire riot is not staged, for once the riot erupts, no one can tell where it will end. Certainly Goldstein can't. One mob in the South of France put two cops in the hospital; it was easy. If you hit a cop over the head with a bench, he'll wind up in the hospital every time.

Anyway, a little spitting by the Masked Man and a small claque in the cheap seats are sufficient to produce a riot, which immediately transforms wrestling from a spectator sport into a participation sport. After that, who can foretell what will happen? Watching, one laughs till his sides ache. But deep down, a man is worried, too; this thing could easily get out of hand.

Bout number four, after the riot is stilled, features a pair of twisting tumbling acrobats. Here are real athletes to watch and admire, while composing oneself to go out into the night.

Robert Lageat is not much taller than Goldstein, but is three times as wide, none of it fat. He is fifty, but looks forty or less. He has loved wrestling all his life. To Lageat, wrestling is an art form. He raised his son to be a wrestler. In 1944 Lageat caught a burst of machine gun fire in the belly. It knocked him into a ravine. He says he got up and ran 1,500 meters holding his guts in his hands. He got away from the Germans, and lived to wrestle again after the war. A companion was killed.

"He wasn't as tough as I," explains Lageat simply. "He wasn't a wrestler."

Lageat's faith in wrestling is humorless. It saved his life; it is worth all a man's devotion. It is the purest and most demanding of the sports: "What else is there? Boxing? Boxing cripples and blinds!"

Lageat boasts of being the last promoter to hire masked wrestlers, the last to present tag-team matches and wrestling girls. He was forced to this by the public—he spits out that word with venom. The public is responsible for what wrestling has become—eccentric, grotesque.

Lageat will not permit the maligning of wrestling in his presence. He will not speak to journalists who plan to treat the sport in an "ironic manner," and when a French television commentator of "ironic" bent came to interview him, Lageat heaved the man over the table. Sometimes, when publicly presenting a card, Lageat will announce that what the mob is about to see is real wrestling, "with nothing tricked up."

"Wrestling is not hokum," Lageat insists. "Is it a joke that men get killed wrestling, that they break bones, lose teeth? Are all those cauliflower ears funny?"

It is true that wrestlers die—of cracked skulls and burst hearts mostly; the effort they expend in a forty-minute bout is astounding. And they do not always land lightly as cats when flung by opponents into the second row. But even Goldstein admits this and is awed by it. "Wrestlers are not like you and me," he murmurs.

Goldstein's masked grapplers changed the game four years ago. Lageat, against his will, was obliged to go along. But apparently he felt that Goldstein's masks were the whole secret. Lageat in turn added only masks, not comedy. Lageat called his men OSS-117, Kamikaze, and the like. "The man gets all his ideas from the titles of movies," says Goldstein disgustedly. "He sees this thing as a wrestler. He's got a very small brain."

In response to Bobby Duranton, Lageat presented the haughty blond giant Jack de Lasartesse—who, like Lageat's masked marvels, never really caught on.

Lageat is infuriated by Duranton's success. "I think he's

disgusting," he says. "He pretends to be a—" Words fail him and he sputters finally, "—a pederast. The man's got children. How will it be when other kids come up to his children and say 'Your father's a famous pederast!' He's disgusting, that's what he is, disgusting."

Lageat says that wrestling in France and Europe boomed for two years in the wake of all the masks and freaks, but that it is failing drastically now, not only for him but for the hated Goldstein too. Goldstein denies this, but Lageat insists it's so. Lageat says it's only a question of time before order reigns again in wrestling, and the good and the true bloom once more.

Lageat is a man drowning in a sea of hokum. It is Goldstein's hokum—Goldstein's inspired hokum.

For two months Goldstein got ready to unmask the White Angel. The White Angel was the purest, most fearless, goodest good guy wrestling had ever known. He was also a marvelous wrestler and a clever comedian and the mob loved him on all levels. He is thirty, Brazilian in origin, and his real name is either Francisco Farina or Pancho Pino, depending on what day you talk to him. Unmasked he is good-looking, and thinks he has a voice. He had already crooned on television, wearing his mask, and now he begged Goldstein to let him strip the mask off so that he could cash in on the White Angel publicity on the stage.

Goldstein finally agreed. For some months the Angel wrestled all over the Continent, having publicly vowed that he would remove his mask if any villain could beat him. Vast throngs turned out half-hoping, half-fearing that their idol would lose. He never did, but he banked plenty of money in the interim, as did Goldstein.

Finally the Angel was matched against the vicious, filthy Masked Man in Paris's Sport Palace, the biggest indoor arena in the country. Win or lose, he would remove his mask after the bout, he said.

The place was packed; two or three thousand fans battled police in the streets, trying to get in. The suspense was twofold: what did the Angel look like; and how would the bout turn out? Goldstein has devised so many bizarre climaxes that the outcome of his bouts is never simply a question of which man will win.

The black-hooded, black-hearted Masked Man was at his most irascible. He kneed, bit and gouged. The fruit began sailing down from the cheap seats: oranges, tomatoes, bananas. And then rotten eggs and cabbages. Lots of cabbages. Wherever this produce struck, it splattered. The frantic evacuation of the ringside seats was pretty funny.

So was what was happening in the ring. The Angel flung the Masked Man out. The huge Masked Man landed on the tiniest photographer anyone had ever seen, crushing him. Ripping off the photographer's camera bag, the Masked Man leaped back into the ring and began lacing the Angel with it.

An old, old lady, her face black with rage, stood on the ring apron beating the Masked Man with her handbag. The Angel was tangled in the ropes and the Masked Man had the Angel's tights half peeled off.

A man can lose his mask with honor, but not his trousers. The Angel broke loose. The two colossi roared at each other from opposite corners of the ring and met head on. The Angel crashed unconscious to the mat; the Masked Man sailed out through the ropes, landed on produce in the now empty ringside seats, and lay there unmoving.

The Angel came to first, and slowly, dramatically, undid his mask.

The audience filed out. The sophisticated ones were weak from mirth, the mental defectives wrung out from the drama of it all. This was Goldstein's chef d'oeuvre. Surely he would not only never be able to surpass it, he would never be able to equal it.

Or so Lageat and the others maintained. "That kind of thing is the negation of sport," explains Lageat stolidly. "You can get away with it once or twice. But there is a limit to a man's imagination. You can't think up something new every time. And when you run out of ideas, you fail. In the long run, pure, disciplined wrestling is what the public wants."

A few weeks later, Goldstein presented a "Heavyweight Tournament." The Masked Man announced in the press that nobody—nobody, you hear—could take his mask off him. He offered 2,000 francs (about $400) to any wrestler in the heavyweight tournament who succeeded.

This was enough to fill the Sports Palace again.

And in the course of the tournament, another wrestler got the Masked Man groggy and tangled in the ropes, and cheered on by thousands of wild-eyed fans, some screaming encouragement, others breathless with excitement, this other wrestler succeeded in removing the Masked Man's mask.

Under it was another mask.

The wrestler could not remove this second mask, as it was glued to the Masked Man's face.

Is there no limit to Goldstein's invention?

"I am fifty-three years old now," Goldstein says. "My imagination is not as prolific as it once was." A quiet smile lights his face and he adds: "But I am confident that I will be able to interest the public for some time to come."

PORTFOLIO 1

GOOD

AND

EVIL

IN

PICTURES

Good looks like this . . .
The purest of the pure,
the imperturbable,
the ineffable *White Angel!*

Evil often wears a mustache and is completely immoral

However, Good, if clean-cut enough, can force
Evil to surrender by tweaking its mustache.

Evil is frequently tattooed, is sometimes seven
feet tall, and when Good gets on Evil's back . . .

Evil doesn't like it at all. (Any wrestler seen
to need a haircut is evil.)

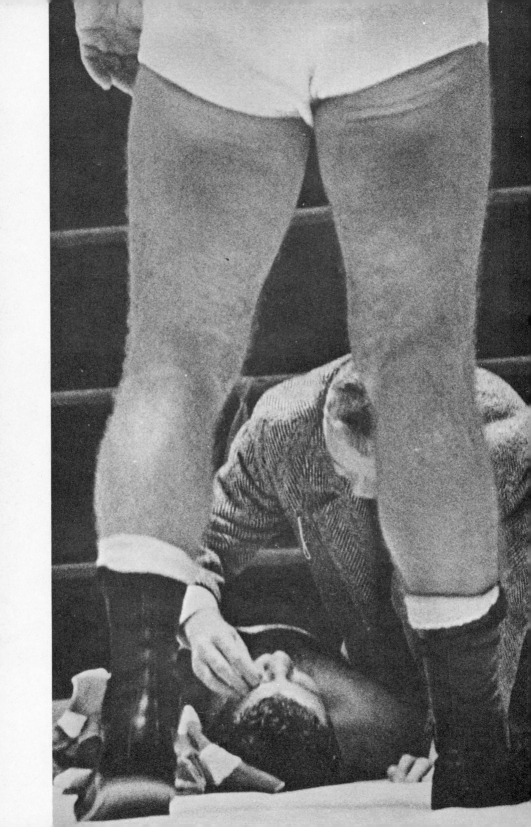

. . . while thousands cheer.

n the end Evil is always (er, almost always)
ft for dead . . .

Unfortunately, villainy, like wrestling,
can never be totally extinguished.

1. Strange as it may seem, the night this photo was taken, the Angel was beaten by Kamikaze, the Suicidal Jap. The Angel succumbed to many vicious fouls because, being pure, he was unable to retaliate in kind.

2. OSS–117, the Secret American Agent in striped trunks, was assaulted by Roger Delaporte. This was after the final bell.

3. The Agent soon mastered cruel Delaporte.

4. Gil Voiney, shown riding Sky-Hi Lee, is world champion (Paris version).

5. Sky is nothing but an evil wrestler; fortunately, he usually gets what's coming to him.

6. André Drapp, villainous Frenchman, lies prostrate, framed by the legs of Lucky Simonovich, a clean-living American. Drapp lay there 30 minutes. I asked Lucky what Drapp was suffering from. Lucky looked startled by the question, but recovered quickly. "I think he dislocated his neck," said he, "or some goddamn thing."

7. The photo was taken at 10:20 P.M. on a Friday night at the Cirque d'Hiver arena in Paris.

8. This is the Masked Man, 6 feet 3 inches, 260 pounds, of hateful immoral profit

5

Gold Panties and Sore Feet

THE LADIES' WORLD

Perhaps there is room in sport for young girls. Perhaps it is good for them to run and jump if they are young enough. But I do not believe there is any room for grown women. There are only two possible *raisons d'être* for sport: to prove who is best, or to earn a living. In the case of women, their "best" is insignificant compared to the performances of men. And in our world they do not, with rare exceptions, earn their living at sport.

But sometimes a woman, too, can be rootless; a tennis racket may be all she has to hold on to. Sometimes a woman, too, can hunger for conquest, for fame. In such cases, a woman becomes as harassed a creature as any male. In the tales which follow, one of the women is a European; the other is an American, but is was Europe which first discovered her and it was to Europe that she kept returning.

If there is no harassment, then there is nothing left to look for except a pretty face. And among lady athletes there are precious few of those.

I Gold Panties

The international tennis set is crowded with displaced

50

persons. There are Czechs and Hungarians who can't go back. There are men who claim no country at all. There are men who have changed nationality so many times that one is afraid to speak to them, not knowing in what tongue they will reply.

In a sense Karol Fageros was a displaced person, too, making the tour because "I like to play tennis and don't know what else to do."

Karol was twenty-five years old and inclined to call Coral Gables, Florida, her home. She had been playing tennis since she was a fat little girl of thirteen. A playmate changed her last name to "Fatros" and sent her running home in tears. Her mother arranged for tennis lessons the next day.

She grew into a big girl, five feet eight, 135 pounds, turned her hair blond, and was invited on her first European tour at eighteen—thanks more to good looks than good tennis. She played in India, Pakistan, Ceylon, Burma, and all through South America and the Caribbean. She also spent a year at the University of Miami, mostly playing tennis and dancing.

She did not win very often. The Canadian women's championship in 1954 was almost her only noteworthy victory, but she was very pretty and no one seemed to mind except Karol herself.

Not until 1958 did Karol hit the big time in a big way— not by winning at Wimbledon, but by being denied admission there because of the gold lamé panties she wore under her tennis outfit. The panties sometimes flashed in the sun when she served. British journalists became terribly flustered in her presence.

"You want to talk about my gold panties, is that it?" Karol would say helpfully.

Karol was helpful and nice to everybody. She was also a curious mixture of the shrewd and the naïve. If she could find some way to set herself apart from other pretty young tennis players, she felt, she might get into the movies, or make a fortune in endorsements.

"Those gold panties made me," Karol said later. "I can get almost anything I want from tournaments now."

But they also ruined the season. "I'd serve, my skirt would fly up and I'd hear someone in the stands snicker, and after that I could hardly hit the ball back any more."

Once rated fifth among American women players, she soon dropped to fourteenth. She also gave up the gold panties, but still owned a dozen outfits, some trimmed in colors, some embodying the chemise-trapeze look.

If she played three matches (singles, doubles, mixed doubles) in an afternoon, she would appear in three different costumes, none of them hiding golden underthings. Nonetheless, foreign crowds continued to whisper about her *culotte extravagante* and leaned forward each time she served, hoping for a flash of reflected sunlight.

Her publicity caused a flicker of interest in Hollywood. Karol was there for four months.

"I had a screen test at Twentieth Century-Fox" she said regretfully, "so I know there's no chance of that."

Most of the four months was spent going to parties, Karol said. She danced with Hugh O'Brian (Wyatt Earp), went horseback riding with Bob Horton (Wagon Train) and dated many other stars. She appeared on television with Groucho Marx, but did poorly in the quiz. "They gave me the booby prize, $50."

On the subject of historical romances or movie magazines, both of which she reads avidly, she might have done better. Her musical knowledge in the dance band field is considerable, too. She also tries to keep up on the latest in gossip columns and clothes.

At Monte Carlo during one tournament she visited the yacht of Aristotle Onassis, the Greek shipping magnate. The yacht is loaded with art treasures. Karol came away unclear about who had painted what, but she glowed about the pink marble bathrooms. One tub was shaped like a whale, she said. The water poured out of a golden faucet like a fish's mouth.

Karol is kind, generous. She is friendly, honest, looks one in the eye as she talks and has a lovely smile. If there had been any meanness in her she might have become a superb player, for she had had an enormous amount of coaching and knew all the shots. But she lacked the killer instinct that makes champions. She did not really want to beat anybody.

"I can't play well against Yola Ramirez," she said once. "I like her too much."

Each tour, Karol insisted, was her last. She had accepted a job managing a dress shop or modeling. She would like to win Wimbledon first—"I photograph well and could make a fortune in endorsements. But I guess I'm not good enough.

"What I would really like to do," she said a bit wistfully "is get married and have children. I'm a home-loving girl, basically."

II Sore Feet

This is a story about the British walking craze and about fame—how it strikes some and ignores others for no apparent reason.

Some months ago men and women all over the British Isles began announcing plans to hike from somewhere to somewhere faster than any pedestrian had gone before. Soon—no one knows why—dozens of persons were marching madly about, claiming new records. Among them was a South African miner named Don Shepherd, forty-three years old, on a holiday. He walked from the southern tip of England to the Scottish border in twenty-one days.

A fifty-six-year-old lady vegetarian known as Dr. Barbara Moore said she could walk from Edinburgh to London on a diet of nuts and carrot juice. She did, and wound up in the hospital suffering from exhaustion.

These were the two principal feats—if you can call them that. About as many people watched the lady doctor as had watched the South African. That is to say, no one.

A group of boys from Kings College seemed to put the craze in perspective when they climbed up and down the steps of the Duke of York monument 641 times, a world record, they claimed, with tongue in cheek. Let's see someone beat that.

The middle-aged Dr. Moore (née Anya Cherkasova) was discharged from the hospital. She resumed hiking, made declarations, gave interviews and avidly pursued the fame that had eluded her all her life.

One day Dr. Moore revealed that she, too, would hike the 1,000-mile length of England. And she began to plod south.

And then a curious thing happened. The South African who had already done this was forgotten and all of Britain, mildly amused up to this point, began to watch Dr. Moore's hiking progress with fascination. Her fame spread even to the Continent, where most newspapers printed daily reports of her march.

The woman is undoubtedly eccentric, the British attitude seemed to be, but she is old enough to be a grandmother and the paper says her bunions are killing her. So she was watched with sympathy, pity, and curiosity.

On and on she hiked—through snow and ice storms, in driving rain. Once she slipped on ice and twisted an ankle. It swelled but she pushed on. Sometimes she fell from exhaustion, was helped to the side of the road, rested awhile, then walked on.

She slept only about four hours a night, ate only fruit and vegetables, and as always, gave interviews during her tea breaks every afternoon.

At last, on a Friday, in the dead of night, she finally reached Land's End. It had taken twenty-three days.

Fireworks, band music, the mayors of six towns and a wildly cheering crowd estimated at ten thousand greeted her arrival. The crowd was so thick she complained that it had trod all over her feet during the last few hundred yards—feet that by then were highly sensitive. She was a heroine at last.

As all of Britain listened, she told in accented English her life story.

She said she had been born in Russia, studied medicine, got in trouble with the secret police, taken a false name and

54

passport, entered a 5,000-mile motorcycle race from Moscow to Tiflis, received a medical degree, got married, and studied shorthand and typing.

It didn't make much sense the way she told it. She had acquired British nationality in 1928 by marrying an Englishman in Moscow and registering with the British Consulate. She never saw her "husband" again, she said.

She was imprisoned in Leningrad in 1933, she said, but Andrei Vishinsky ordered her released. She made her way to England in 1934 via motorcycle races in Berlin and Switzerland. She spoke no English then but in 1944 she published a book called, "I Am a Woman from Soviet Russia." Hardly anyone read it.

She said she had cured herself of leukemia by dieting. No one listened. She entered an air race but did not win. Finally she hit on hiking about the country, and at fifty-six, found herself famous at last.

She owes much of her success, she said, to her pet tortoise, Fangio.

"It was from Fangio that I learned how to cut my breathing down to four a minute," she said. "Normally, human beings breathe sixteen times a minute."

Today she is a celebrity all over England. Officials of her town firmly rejected a suggestion that her achievement be commemorated, but what does she care? She is famous, they are not. She snorted and said she would be remembered long after they are all dead.

6

Mob Rule

THE WORLD OF SOCCER

In Europe soccer is rarely called soccer. In England it is football, in France it is the same word with a French accent. In Spain it is El Futbol. In many other countries it is the same word with slight variations. It is the only game played which has an enormous international following, and a real fan in any one country can give you the pedigrees of stars in any other country. In most countries, attendance is on a gradual decline, although for specific matches crowds are as big and frantic as ever. Fans seem to be getting bored with their own teams, but they will still pay heavily to see some foreign team with a famous new star. There is a busy trade in players back and forth across the borders and the best soccer is played in whichever country currently has the most lax recruiting laws. Most countries limit foreign players to one or two per team. So when a foreign star is purchased he is "urged" to become a citizen of his new country, and his "request" for citizenship is processed at once. Then he is not a foreigner any more, and a new foreign player can be brought in. Spain had the most foreigners and the best teams during the fifties, but now Italy seems to lead.

Soccer is very big in Europe, but appears to have little

56

emotional punch. People go to the matches, but they are more likely to talk about, say, a bike race. Except of course for a juicy "manifestation" of which soccer currently is so full.

I Bad Dreams

Let's say that you are the soccer promoter in Turin, Italy. Your traditional rival, Inter of Milan, comes to town in the waning days of the season. Milan is in third place, only a game behind Turin, which is leading the league. Milan is your natural rival, anyway. This game is crucial and you have a sellout on your hands. Do you rub your hands with glee and hire an armored truck to carry the money to the bank?

Perhaps you do. But wait—don't be so hasty.

Your stadium holds 75,000 persons. You have a season subscription of 10,000. You put the other 65,000 tickets on sale and they are snapped up within a day. You bank 105 million lire — $175,000 — which is a lot of money in any language.

Game day dawns. It is raining, but the money is already in the bank, so what do you care?

Everywhere you go that Sunday morning, however, people are talking about the game. You are not innocent, you have known the sight of Italian soccer fans gone berserk. So you feel a bit nervous.

The stadium is packed long before game time. Fans sit in the rain. In their passion to see the game, there are probably many who don't even realize that it is pouring.

Mobs of angry fans mill about the street. You get more and more nervous.

Suddenly the rush starts. More than 10,000 men storm the gates. Hundreds scale the walls. Gatekeepers are punched, pummeled, and trampled. More hundreds go over the walls.

You watch all this, sick inside, and there is not a thing you can do about it.

There are 10,000 of them. They know exactly what they want and a trained army could not do it better.

How can you stop 10,000 men? You can't shoot them, and if you had 10,000 policemen on hand (which you don't) it would not be enough.

The ever-swelling mob surrounds the field, blocking the view of patrons who have paid, and threatening violence to the players from Milan.

Milan scores. The crowd feels that a Turinese defender was taken out of the play. It gets angry and invades the playing field. The game is stopped. The public address announcer coaxes most of the mob off the field and the game begins once more.

Minutes later, the mob is milling over the field again. The Milan team races for its locker room. There are rioters everywhere. The public address can hardly be heard. The rain pours down.

The home team trudges back onto the field after the announcer has coaxed part of the mob behind the sidelines. Under the stands, an official pleads frantically with Milan to take the field. Milan refuses. It isn't safe, for one thing. For another, Milan need only sit tight to win this important game by forfeit.

After ninety minutes of mob rule, the referee calls off the game. You, if you are the promoter, get ready to pay back that $175,000.

Your heart isn't in it, though.

It took only a day to collect all that money, but it takes a week to repay it. The long lines move slowly up to the windows day after day.

You plead with the Soccer Federation not to award the game to Milan by forfeit. You plead that it is not your fault that your guards and ticket takers were snowed under by 10,000 persons. You produce photographs of hundreds of men and boys scaling the walls.

You plead poverty and sincerity too. You have just reimbursed $175,000 and you look pretty sick.

This has never happened before and the league cannot decide. It declares it will render its verdict in ten days. You promise meekly to add another 30,000 places to your stadium if you are spared.

This is a game you could not afford to lose. Now you must wait ten full days for the axe to fall, reimbursing thousands of dollars every day, waiting to lose a game because of a broken rule and the fanaticism of 10,000 loyal fans.

Worst of all, you have bad dreams almost every night. What can you do if 10,000 persons assault your gates again? What can you ever possibly do?

II Whistling in the Dark

The world's loudest noise?

Try listening to the harsh, derisive whistling of 100,000 or more soccer fans when Club Real of Madrid plays Barcelona in Madrid. The whistling is colossal in size, unending in duration, skull-splitting in shrillness.

The whistling swells and swells, sustained for minutes on end. It is ear-piercing, deafening, and scrapes nerves raw.

Barcelona and Madrid are not only natural rivals, they often are the two strongest teams in European soccer. For a week before matches in Madrid, trains, planes, and buses from Barcelona are jammed. An estimated 25,000 fans come from Barcelona to see the match. Stay-at-home fans send a deluge of telegrams, up to fifteen hundred in all, wishing the team luck.

Madrid fans normally spend the week buying whistles. Long before game day none are left in Madrid shops. Still, comparatively few in the packed stadium (capacity 125,000) have them. Most whistling during the game is of the two-finger-in-the-mouth variety.

The insulting whistling starts as Barcelona players take the field. It never stops except for half-time.

It varies in intensity. But every time Barcelona drives downfield the whistling swells again, louder and shriller than ever, until an observer's nerves are twanging like bowstrings and he imagines his brain about to burst.

The Barcelona players seem bowed down by all that noise. The noise completely submerges their own rooters, submerges also the one puny whistle of the referee. Most years the referee manages to keep order somehow. If he didn't, there could easily be bloodshed.

The point is, the national sport in Spain is not bullfighting; it is soccer. Bullfighting in Spain is for tourists and also for the peasants who come in from the country to the summer fiestas and blow a year's savings in one wild week. The business deals of bullfighting are conducted in bars and all transactions are in cash. The bullfighters leave town after each fight carrying paper parcels full of money. Socially, bullfighting is the equivalent of prizefighting and few Spaniards above the rank of, say, hotel clerk will admit having anything to do with it. Instead, they insist that the bulls these days are as docile as cattle, and that the matadors charlatans all, and that they themselves never attend fights.

But soccer draws men, women, and children to the stadiums in enormous numbers. The Barcelona-Real Madrid gate has totaled as much as 7,000,000 pesetas (about $116,000).

Soccer even shows signs of cracking Spain's rigid isolationism. Not only are Barcelona and Real Madrid in demand everywhere, but so are television broadcasts of their matches. The European Cup match between Real Madrid and Nice in 1959 was televised by Eurovision. It was the first television program ever to cross the Pyrenees into the rest of Europe.

III The Big Gun

It was the grayest day in the history of Paris's Racing Club soccer team. Not only did Racing lose to Rouen, 1–0, before one of the biggest home crowds of the season, but it also lost the receipts from the match, about $18,000. The money never reached the bank. As he had done after every match for five years Emile Baujoin, the club's treasurer, tossed two sacks of money into his car, climbed in beside his wife, and drove toward a bank—five minutes away from the Parc des Princes Stadium by city streets.

This time, two other club officials were in the back seat. The bank had been telephoned to expect the treasurer's car, and two employees waited to open the bank doors when Baujoin and his two sacks of money appeared.

The occupants of the car were glum as they drove along. The lost match was on everybody's mind.

Baujoin pulled up beside the bank.

Before he could open the door, something smashed through the back window of the car. A hammer, some of the car's occupants said later. A revolver butt, said others.

Baujoin, turning, found himself staring down the barrel of a machine gun.

There were three men, all masked. Two carried machine guns, the other a pistol.

"The dough, quick," one man cried, "or I'll burn your brains."

Baujoin's wife screamed, "Stop thief!" And then, "We're being robbed!"

Baujoin stared at the machine gun and handed over the money.

Inside the bank, a man already was telephoning the police.

The three thieves leaped into a car and drove away. It was 6:00 P.M. and dark. It is not clear whether anybody got the number of the car or not. A number was given to the police by Baujoin and the others; apparently the car with that number belonged to a prominent industrialist of Paris, a man who owns several companies.

Baujoin said the robbers were young.

"The money sacks weighed over forty pounds," he said. "The guy had his machine gun under one arm and the sacks under the other, but sprinted to his car like a dash man."

This is the only clue police had to go on: the head thief was young and athletic. It is not, they have been explaining to club officials ever since, very much.

Baujoin submitted to interviews all the next day and by

evening his patience was wearing thin. Someone asked him why, although his wife screamed for help, he didn't make a sound himself.

"Nobody was pointing a machine gun at my wife," replied Baujoin acidly.

Officials of the Racing team were also asked by about a hundred cops and reporters why the receipts weren't insured. Too expensive, they replied sadly. Why had Baujoin been allowed to go five years without varying his routine by more than a few seconds?

To this question there was no answer at all.

Nearly everybody was convinced that the robbers had been planning the holdup for months, and that probably they were fanatical fans of the team. They knew the routine too well to be casual crooks. They even had it planned for this Sunday, obviously knowing that the crowd would be exceptionally large. Racing was second place, Rouen fourth. The crowd numbered 23,893.

The puzzle then became: How could they do such a thing to a team they probably love?

Early the next morning, the empty sacks were found by a night watchman on his rounds far across the city. The head thief must have had an ironic sense of humor, for he tossed them over the fence into the confines of another bank.

IV Riot

When riots erupt at soccer matches (as they do regularly in Italy, for example) it is often quite funny—unless you happen to be the unfortunate referee or players trapped by the mob. But now a riot has occurred that is not funny at all. It did not take place because of any penchant for disorder. It did not take place in Italy, where bad behavior by fans has become such an ingrained habit that persons attending matches are no longer held responsible for their acts.

This particular riot occurred strictly because of chauvinism

—or nationalism—the current curse of sport. It came about because of the inability of peoples to understand each other and to communicate.

In the semi-final round of the European Cup soccer tournament, Benfica, the Portuguese champion, played Rapid of Vienna, the Austrian champion, at Vienna.

They had already played at Lisbon. The Portuguese won that game 3–0. Now, to qualify for the Cup final, Vienna would have to win this second game by four goals or more. Against a team as strong as the Portuguese, this was asking for a miracle, and every fan in Vienna knew it.

Nevertheless, 63,000 fans packed Vienna's Prater Stadium to see the match. All knew after half an hour of play that there would be no miracle. The Portuguese defense was impenetrable. The Portuguese offense blasted in another goal. Now Vienna needed four goals to force a third match and five to qualify for the final. But only twenty-two minutes remained. That is not nearly enough time for so many goals, but it's plenty for disgraceful conduct by Vienna's players and fans alike.

For some time the fans had been hooting and whistling at every move by Portugal. They had cursed and excoriated the referee, an Englishman named Leafe. They had encouraged every show of temper by their own players, cheered deliberate fouls and mocked Portuguese surprise.

Now the Vienna players took heart from this, and began kicking shins instead of the ball. They slugged, butted, and charged. Pursuit of the ball became a pretext for assaulting Portuguese players.

Little by little the bewildered Portuguese began to retaliate, and soon there were fist fights on all parts of the field. Referee Leafe admonished certain players, but since he spoke neither Portuguese nor German, this did not accomplish much.

Instead of listening, players surrounded him, punched him, spat on him. The Viennese fans cheered more vociferously for their team as the game deteriorated. The Viennese goal tender left his goal and ran about slugging Portuguese players.

Leafe was powerless. For a while longer he tried to save the game, but now fans were milling about the field, too. Leafe ran for the dressing room. The game was over.

For an hour and a half, mob rule prevailed in the stadium. No one left. Police reinforcements arrived, but were blocked off by portions of the angry mob. Everything in the stadium that could be destroyed was destroyed: benches, signs, lights, concession stands.

A police armored car succeeded in rescuing Leafe from his dressing room. After three hours, a police bus finally got the Portuguese players out of their dressing room. The sated crowd finally began to disperse.

Observers said that never in any stadium in Europe had they seen such violence, such savagery and such stupidity. And yet, the Portuguese had committed no crime at all—unless it is a crime at such a time and place to be highly skilled and non-Austrian.

Worse, one wonders what hope there is for understanding among nations if even sportsmanship—the game itself—cannot curb animosity among nations, cannot smother this terrible urge for national supremacy.

One wonders if Americans could behave this way, too. Soccer in the United States does not enjoy the popularity it has in other nations. But if it had that popularity, would American fans, on occasion, demonstrate against foreign teams? Would we, too, in a burst of national outrage, forget the game to riot and destroy, as Europeans and South Americans so often do?

7

From Cobblestones To Jets

THE WORLD OF
EUROPEAN HORSE RACING

IN America horse racing is simply horse racing. But in Europe it has its head in the door of a transoceanic airliner and its roots deep in the Middle Ages. And so cobblestone piazzas sometimes frame horse racing, as do entire villages with surrounding forests, and also, sometimes, the sweat and blood of highly paid press agents.

I The Slugging Jocks

Siena's Palio of the Contrade may rank as the most electrifying of all European spectacles.

The Palio, held twice each year (on July 2 in honor of Our Lady of Provenzano, and on August 15 for the Feast of the Assumption) is a wild and woolly horse race straight out of the Middle Ages. The horses, selected by lot, represent ten sections of the city, and the race around the cobblestone piazza in the heart of downtown, symbolizes the potentially violent rivalries among the sections.

Medieval tactics prevail—and have prevailed since the first Palio in the thirteenth century. The jockeys ride bareback, their skulls protected by steel helmets shaped like deerstalker caps. These helmets are essential because the Palio is not so much a horse race as a slugging contest among the jockeys.

They go at each other with their whip handles while galloping along at top speed over the cobbles. If one jockey cannot shake another by clubbing him off his horse, all is not lost. He can ride the other into the wall of a building and stop him that way.

The race is fought in the huge Piazza del Campo, which is shaped like a giant seashell, but tilted so that the horses not only must navigate two right angle corners, but also must plunge downhill over the cobbles, and then scramble up again.

There is no whopping amount of prize money to be won; the prize is a silk banner bearing a hand-painted image of the Virgin. About $25,000 is involved but it is raised by supporters of the various entrants and paid out in bribes.

To insure the victory of a particular steed, dozens of persons must be reached—owners and jockeys of all the other horses, as well as determined citizens who might consider countering your bribes with bribes of their own. Then you must set a guard on your own jockey to make sure no one gets to him, and a guard on your guard, and so on.

Nobody can be trusted in Siena during Palio week. Hordes of tourists double the population of the city (55,400), to watch the race. They must more or less shift for themselves for no true citizen of Siena has time for anything but the skulduggery. Honor itself is at stake.

Final deals are sealed in the dark of the night before the race. At dawn, the town is fraught with suspense. So much corruption has gone on that no one is sure who has managed to fix whom.

All ten *contrade* repair to their local churches dragging the horses with them.

Later there is a blessing of all the horses by the archbishop in the great cathedral, a board floor having been put down to keep the hoofs from marking the mosaic. Thousands watch as holy water is thrown on the beasts. If one of the horses should forget his manners while in church, this is considered not sacrilege, but the best possible kind of good luck. While the sacristan goes for a shovel, everyone else rushes outside to bet on that horse.

When the parade begins in the piazza at 5:00 P.M. all seats are taken and the huge infield is packed. Women faint, are passed over the crowd, and rushed, limp and unconscious, to first-aid stations. At least a dozen are carried out each year. More than seventy thousand persons watch the Palio.

Each contrada parades in turn, led by its flag-wavers, who perform dozens of intricate movements in tandem. This includes hurling the flag furled into the air so that it opens outlined against the sky, falls, and is caught. The flag-wavers are followed by young men in medieval finery. Then there is a knight in armor astride a horse, then the race horse led by a boy.

The costumed paraders wear wigs and the faces under them seem like faces out of Botticelli. The knight in armor in each contradal unit is the jockey who will shortly ride in the race. Most jockeys seem annoyed by the parade and anxious to get on with the race. Usually one communicates his nervousness to his steed. Skittish already, it sheds its bridle, then its knight in armor. The medieval wig goes one way and the armor with the knight in it goes another. Clang!

At last the race horses approach the start. They are ordinary horses but were selected a month ago and have been fed and groomed till they shine like thoroughbreds.

Favorites are, say, entries from the Tower, Caterpillar, and Goose sections of the town. The Tower horse, running for a different contrada then, had won an earlier race and is the odds-on choice.

The race does not start with high-strung steeds darting out of neat little gates. The starter simply touches a match to some loose gunpowder, which goes POOF!—nearly blowing up the town. The horses then leap over or become entangled in the rope that has held them back. Sometimes jockeys will jump off their horses and start slugging one another with whip handles. In any case, the race is on, and one is soon able to tell in which direction the heaviest bribery points.

The piazza is about twice the size of the town's great medieval cathedral and the race is three laps. The first horse to finish is the winner, whether there is anyone riding him or not. More than one riderless horse has won the Palio.

Often, persons in the crowd will yank a jockey off the horse as it goes by. Sometimes the jockey will then stand in the track and unseat as many fellow riders as he can in the remaining laps—whether to fulfill his end of a bribe or merely for spite is difficult to say.

Half the spectators are locals who, in a little more than a minute, manage to shout themselves hoarse, and half are tourists who have not the slightest idea what is happening.

Jockeys race with one eye on the track, one on other jockeys whom they are busily clobbering with their whips. The braver jockeys careen into each turn. The careful ones slow to get round, like race cars downshifting for a corner.

After two laps, the Tower horse, the favorite, seems a certain winner, whereupon a gray nag nearly a lap behind turns broadside into the track, his jockey jumping off and running for the fence. Tower and one other horse strike the gray, catapulting their riders into the sky.

On the last lap Caterpillar and Goose are neck and neck. The Goose jockey tries to wrestle his horse to the cobblestones, and gets heaved by it into the wall of a building. He gets up and wobbles toward the finish line, where Caterpillar has already won.

The Caterpillar jockey is carried off to safety by his adoring fans. If losers had got to this fellow, they would have killed him or so the Sienese claim to believe.

An elderly Englishwoman stands up and says: "They're all mad here, quite mad."

That seems to describe it.

All is not over. The victorious contrada can be depended upon to go boasting and taunting through the streets beginning about 9:00 P.M. And soon there will be hundreds of fist fights breaking out all over town. Sport, of one kind or another, lasts all night.

II English Enclave

It is 6:00 A.M., raining, and the race horses plod down the street toward the forest that surrounds the village. Their hoofs go clip-clop on the street. Small boys perched atop the saddles huddle into themselves against the rain. They wear turtlenecked sweaters and peaked caps, and they hold their heads down under the cold dawn drizzle.

There are houses along both sides of the street with trees along the sidewalks, and then the pavement ends, the forest closes in upon the village, and the race horses enter it and are covered by the dripping trees. The trees are chestnuts, oaks, and sometimes willows, and they are red, brown, and yellow. The autumn colors are dull in the rain, and the narrow paths through the forest over which the horses gallop lie under a moist blanket of fallen leaves.

This is the village of Chantilly, seven thousand men, women, and children, and fifteen hundred race horses. Chantilly, twenty-five miles north of Paris, is dedicated to the race horse. It houses about twenty training establishments, stabling between fifty and a hundred horses each, plus the stately homes of owners and trainers, and some expensive restaurants which serve exquisitely cooked game.

There are four training areas, one of them the great, beautiful forest of Chantilly. The forest is interlaced by sand-covered tracks which run dead straight under the trees for two miles or more.

There are twenty miles of gallops tunneling through the forest and it is here that most of the fifteen hundred horses work out each dawn. At l'Aigle, across the village, another 575 acres are available, most of them a grassy plain with straights two miles long as well.

Then there is the jewel-like Chantilly race course, with a medieval château rising out of the back stretch, a lovely little grandstand, and the betting windows ranged alongside under the trees. The track is grass, so carefully tended that it is always bright green, with very white rails. The whole of this, château included, is surrounded by the forest. There are meetings on this course only six days a year.

About one hundred and twenty groundskeepers are employed. Many work mainly at night, readying the gallops for the dawn workouts.

Chantilly is the seat of French racing—the only racing in the world, by the way, which shows a profit. The average French race horse earns about $200 a month more than he costs.

Horse racing came to France from England about 1830, and the first track was the Champ de Mars, where the Eiffel Tower is now. A training center was needed and the Duc de Morny, half-brother to the Emperor, suggested Chantilly, famous for its stag hunting.

The English invasion hit Chantilly almost at once—trainers and horses first, then grooms and stable boys, many of whom were shanghaied out of London pubs when drunk or drugged and sold across the Channel by unscrupulous relatives or bartenders.

Then came English noblemen and horse owners, then devoted English horseplayers, then English bookmakers to make betting as easy as at home. Lastly, to save all these lost souls, came English parsons avid to build English churches and stamp out sin. Chantilly had Anglican and Methodist Churches long before most of the rest of France, and has them to this day.

By 1900, more than half the population of Chantilly was English. But nowadays few English are left. Trainers still have names like Jack Cunnington, Alec Head and Percy Carter, but most of them are third or fourth generation and French nationals now. Though most speak English, their British passports lapsed ages ago.

Many of the grooms and stablehands, though French, are bilingual also. They speak perfect French, of course. They also speak Cockney English as it was spoken in the streets of London before 1850.

So Chantilly is, in a way, a foreign enclave of the type which was common in Europe centuries ago, but which is a very strange thing now. It is a beautiful place with beautiful horses galloping through the forest under the trees.

III Getting the Horse's Goat

The airlifting of the European horse to America for important races is a routine thing today, unless you happen to be paying the bills—$2,500 per horse—or are worried about what horses might do at high altitude. Everybody says that shipments are always accompanied by a man with a gun, whose job is to shoot anything which starts kicking a hole in the side of the plane 30,000 feet over the Atlantic. Every time this anecdote is recounted, the listeners always laugh. I have never been able to find out if the story is true or not. Is that guy with the gun really aboard?

Anyway, it is the loading of horses at the European end, and getting them off at the other, that grays the hair of track owners and their press agents.

One owner (female) refuses at the last minute to send her horse to America. She has just learned that those mean American health officials plan to inoculate the beast upon arrival. She refuses to let anyone cause her precious any pain. The plane's engines are already turning over. The track owner flatters her, pleads with her. Even the pilot comes out to help.

A jockey from East Germany, stalwart member of his country's Communist party, can't get a visa. The jockey says his horse isn't going without him. Would a little bribery change his mind? If so, how much?

But the all-time classic was the tale of Kracovie, fastest trotting mare in Europe, and her inseparable pal Brigitte, a sheep (or was it a goat?).

Brigitte lived in Kracovie's stall, traveled about Europe in Kracovie's van, and was loved by Kracovie with an insane and devoted love. Brigitte was an ornery creature which charged any towel, rag, or photographer like a fighting bull. Nobody other than Kracovie's owner, Raoul van Rillas, and driver, Roger Vercruyesse, got close enough to know what it looked like. Van Rillas told Roosevelt Raceway (Westbury, Long Island) that Brigitte was a sheep. He said that Kracovie had been a mediocre horse before Brigitte moved in, but since then had won nine of fourteen races and the European circuit championship. He had since tried to leave Brigitte behind once or twice; the horse had promptly refused to eat, or even to train.

Van Rillas told Roosevelt representatives it was absolutely essential that Brigitte accompany the horse to America. This was fine with Roosevelt, which felt it could make much publicity capital of the horse with the inseparable sheep. Accordingly, plans were made to fly Brigitte to America in the same plane with Kracovie and one other horse.

Brigitte, described in Roosevelt publicity as a sheep, was listed on the custom's manifest as a sheep. Alitalia Airlines agreed to transport a sheep. United States Public Health officials publicly stated that the welcome mat was out to any French sheep which cared to make the trip.

The only thing the Public Health Department won't accept is goats.

The day before the flight, M. Van Rillas displayed Brigitte to three American sportswriters outside of Kracovie's Paris barn. The three were all New Yorkers born and bred, and Mr. Joe Goldstein, representing Roosevelt Raceway, is from Brooklyn. All four agreed that Brigitte was a fine-looking sheep.

Then one of the newsmen remembered that sheep were supposed to have wool.

"Where's Brigitte's wool?" he asked.

"We shaved it off for the warm weather," answered Van Rillas suavely. The reporter nodded at the wisdom of this, and apologized for having asked a stupid question.

One of the newsmen spoke a little French. He asked the driver, Vercruyesse, what Brigitte was.

Vercruyesse does not speak English. *"Une chèvre,"* he replied.

The newsmen thumbed frantically through dictionaries, where *"chèvre"* is invariably translated as "goat."

Van Rillas spoke sharply to the driver in French, then smiled at the newsmen and remarked easily: "You mustn't pay any attention to that driver. He knows a lot about horses. He just doesn't know anything about sheep."

"If you ask me, it's no sheep."

Now the newsmen were murmuring among themselves.

"Looks like a goat."

"If you ask me, it's no sheep."

"I'm nearly sure it's a goat."

Mr. Joe Goldstein, responsible for getting the horse to Roosevelt Raceway, with or without Brigitte, was perspiring profusely.

"For the time being, fellows," he said, "let's call it a sheep, okay?"

The next afternoon Mr. Goldstein received a phone call from Alitalia Airlines.

"Are you prepared to prove that this animal is a sheep?" a voice demanded.

"I could almost swear it's a sheep," said Mr. Goldstein nervously. "I mean, I'm practically convinced of it."

He hurried out to the airport fearing the worst.

Very little runs on schedule in Europe. The flight was scheduled to take off at eight o'clock that night. Then it was postponed to 2:00 A.M. This was fine with M. Van Rillas, as Paris is a very dark place at 2:00 A.M. The darker the better.

At the airport, Alitalia officials loaded sulkies, hay, pitchforks, and assorted other gear onto the DC-7. The horses and Brigitte waited in closed vans. The horses were eating oats, and Brigitte was munching a newspaper.

At about 3:30 A.M., instructions finally were given to load the animals through a door in the front of the plane. This is a door that humans must stoop to enter. Brigitte, though remarkably tall for a sheep, could have made it, but not the horses.

"How do you expect us to get the horses through that door?" asked M. Van Rillas testily.

"Just have them bend down a little," he was told.

It took more than two hours to unload the plane so that the

horses could enter through the rear. By this time the sky had turned pink and a sleepy photographer was able to snap photos without a flash.

M. Van Rillas must have realized that the jig was up as he led Brigitte from the van to the plane.

All of the officials present were very polite. They told him that although Brigitte was undoubtedly a sheep, as he said, sheep that looked like goats weren't allowed either.

M. Van Rillas, his wife near tears, declared angrily that Kracovie wasn't going to New York without that sheep.

Mr. Goldstein was really nervous now. For the next hour he gave a remarkable demonstration of tact, diplomacy, and fast talking.

"Furthermore," Mr. Goldstein announced finally, seizing inspiration where he found it, "we'll not only find another sheep —er, Brigitte-type animal—in New York, but we'll have it meet the plane so that she and Kracovie can get acquainted at once."

Mme. Van Rillas dried her eyes. She said that she was very mad at the United States Government, Roosevelt Raceway, Alitalia and whoever owns Orly Airport, but not at Mr. Goldstein. Kracovie could go to New York.

Mr. Goldstein gave a vast sigh, then signaled the pilot to start the engines quick!

In parting, Mr. Goldstein promised that in a few days M. Van Rillas should probably be able to convince all parties that Brigitte was really a sheep after all. Inasmuch as Brigitte is the only sheep in the world which can butt a man ten feet into the air, this last promise of Mr. Goldstein was stretching it a bit.

Brigitte never did get to New York. Kracovie finished second in the race, then was flown back to Paris where horse and goat were tearfully reunited. And they lived happily ever after.

8

Guides and Climbers

THE WORLD OF MOUNTAINS

IF Europe were flat its history might be less contorted, and certainly its sport would be. The mountains are the backbone of the sport of the Continent. The bike races and all the auto rallies go over them. Race cars climb them. Skiers and bob-sledders plunge down them at tremendous speed. People hunt and fish and ride in them, and most of all Alpinists scramble up them, or die trying. The sport of Europe is graphically different from the sport of the United States, and perhaps the Alps are the major reason. In America, sport was a settled thing before anyone lived out as far as the Rocky Mountains. Our sporting culture is the culture of a flat country, or at worst a country of gently rolling hills. As a country, we have never known the violent struggle, the violent accidents, that go on when men pit themselves against the peaks.

I The Guide

The most sobering aspect of Zermatt, Switzerland, is not the majesty of its great peaks, but a stroll through its cemetery. It is a cemetery stuffed with dead climbers, young men and women from every corner of Europe, from Brazil, Ireland, America, India.

75

Inscriptions on the tombstones read: "Departed To A Better Life From The Slopes Of The Matterhorn At Dawn, July 25 . . ." Or: "Fell From The Monte Rosa After Reaching The Summit . . ."

In one tomb repose three young Englishmen who had been roped together. No one will ever know which brought the others down with him. Beside lie the remains of an unknown climber found by guides who went up to recover the Englishmen.

There are a dozen peaks ringing Zermatt, the most famous of which is the 14,701-foot pyramid of rock and ice known as the Matterhorn. It is not the tallest mountain in Europe, nor even in this group. But it is renowned for its surpassing beauty and because it has killed over a hundred men, including four of the first seven to scale it.

Climbing mountains is probably the world's most perilous recreation. Each summer about 250 persons are killed in the Alps from France to Austria. Most are very young (between eighteen and twenty-three), completely inexperienced, and climb guideless. The majority fall, often dragging pals down, too, but a few get lost crossing glaciers and are frozen solid before anyone finds them. Professional guides could have prevented most of the first type accidents, and all of the second.

For many years there were an even hundred diplomaed guides in Zermatt who were kept busy all summer by a clientele which was mostly British. But for some reason the British seem to have given up the sport. These days there is more climbing than in the past, but the climbers now are predominantly German, and the Germans rarely hire guides.

(Similarly, German tourists flood all of Europe, but do not bring prosperity with them because they seem to prefer camping to staying in hotels, picnicking to dining in restaurants.)

In any case there are now only about thirty-five guides in Zermatt, and no young ones putting in the required two years as a mountain porter, before the diploma is awarded and the new guide trusted with a tourist.

A typical guide is Adolf Schaller, thirty-one years old.

Schaller became a porter at nineteen, and has been a guide since twenty-one. Each summer he scales the Matterhorn about twenty times.

"Everyone wants to climb the Matterhorn," he says. "There are better mountains here, but no one is interested in them."

In all he has climbed that one mountain over one hundred times. His fee, set by the guides' union, is the equivalent of $33 for the two-day ascent.

Like all the guides, Schaller teaches skiing in winter. Financially, winter is a better season than summer. In the spring and fall, when there are no tourists in Zermatt, Schaller must work as a laborer or carpenter on building projects, if he wants to go on eating.

In a good year he may earn $2,500, perhaps a third of it while clinging to the face of a mountain, attached by rope to tourists who are, to a greater or lesser degree, inept. Schaller does not consider that climbing is work.

"If the client should fall," he says, "the guide must be able to hold him."

Hundreds of persons scale the Matterhorn each summer. The record is supposed to be 114 in a single day.

The Matterhorn was conquered for the first time on July 14, 1865, by a party of seven led by the Englishman Edward Whymper, then twenty-five. On the way down a rope broke and four men plunged to their deaths.

Whymper never got over that. He hung about the Alps the rest of his life, climbing them, photographing them, deep-set eyes haunted by what they had seen. He died at seventy-one, still brooding about the sheer, terrifying face of the peak he called "that awful mountain."

II The Man Who Climbed the Matterhorn—Almost

This is the story of a tourist who decided to climb the Matterhorn.

He liked the idea very much. It would make swell conversation at cocktail parties back in the States; he would be seeing

77

"a part of Europe the average tourist never sees," and it pleased him to think of himself as bold and fearless, an Alpinist with nerves of steel.

The Matterhorn, a colossal arrowhead which thrusts upward from the valley floor to 14,701 feet, has an ugly reputation, but the tourist felt certain that this was exaggerated.

Someone once told him that the Matterhorn was a "ladies' " mountain these days. Everyone climbed it. The tourist preferred to believe this verson. Surely the Swiss had removed all risk from the mountain by now. Everyone knows how accommodating the Swiss are.

Accordingly, the tourist arrived in Zermatt and engaged a guide.

"How tough is the climb?" he asked.

"Nothing to it," replied the guide, who, this late in the season, had not had a client in several days and was not going to scare one off if he could help it.

As the guide explained things, the cost would be about $50, most of it the guide's fee. The climb would take two days. The tourist needed no equipment except boots.

"Are you in good shape?" asked the guide.

The tourist had been considered a fair athlete in college nearly ten years earlier. He had not yet started to put on weight or lose hair so he answered: "Yes, quite good shape."

They arranged to meet at 3:00 P.M. Having several hours to kill, the tourist wandered through the village museum, which was stuffed with mementos of grisly accidents of the past, such as shredded climbing ropes and clothing punctured in many places by sharp rocks.

After that, he went for a turn around the cemetery. His confidence began to wane when he counted the graves of sixty-nine climbers; the Matterhorn had accounted for most of them.

At 3:00 P.M., he and the guide hiked up to the funicular, which lifted them in a few minutes to 7,700 feet, eliminating what used to be the first four hours of the climb. Leaving the car, they trudged up a gradually steepening slope toward the hut at nearly 11,000 feet where they would spend the night.

The late sun was on the encircling peaks and the glaciers that fell from them were in shadow. The glaciers were black with a coating of dirt. They were ugly.

It grew cold, windy, and harder to breathe as guide and tourist neared the hut. Ahead and above, the Matterhorn rose stark, black, awesome. Close up it looked even steeper. The tourist was beginning to feel nervous.

After several hours, they reached the hut. Other climbers already were there, and they sat around a wood-burning stove drinking coffee. At about seven, two women who live all summer in the hut served a dinner of soup, pot roast, dark bread, and wine.

About 8:00 P.M., fully dressed except for boots, the tourist wrapped himself in three blankets in a bunk and tried to sleep. Several times in the night he awoke suddenly, as if from a nightmare. He kept thinking about how steep the mountain looked. His heart was thumping.

Before dawn, someone lit a candle in the bunkroom, and he began to tug on boots. Breakfast was coffee and coarse bread. Outside it was dark. The guide asked how he felt. The tourist peered nervously up at the dark bulk of the mountain, and said he felt all right.

The guide roped them together, slung his pack, and they started up. The Matterhorn rose straight up, a wall of broken rock. As they climbed in the night, the tourist was trying to convince himself that he trusted the guide completely.

Then the guide fell. Scrambling frantically, he caught himself. At the other end of the rope, clinging to the mountain by his fingernails, the tourist had been thinking: "I hope he doesn't expect me to stop him."

It began to be dawn. They went on, clambering up the sheer face of the Matterhorn, the rock slippery with a coating of frost. The tourist's old army boots kept slipping. The wind blew. He was scared. Looking down, he understood why the mountain had killed so many and wondered why it hadn't killed more.

Panting from exertion and thin air, he asked the guide when the mountain got less steep.

"It doesn't," said the guide. "I thought you knew."

They kept climbing up. The tourist could not catch his breath. His knees were trembling, whether from fatigue or fright he didn't know. In an hour, they had climbed a precarious 1,000 feet. Three hours more up to the summit. If he got there, how would he ever get down again?

It was light enough to see the valley two miles below. The tourist began to long for his wife and children, the taste of good wine, the smell of the sea. Fingers searching for holds, he climbed a little higher.

"This," he said suddenly, "is fantastically dangerous. I'm going down. There's nothing up there I want. I'm going down."

He took the first train out of Zermatt. He watched the mountain from the window, the "easy mountain," the "ladies' mountain."

He had never been so glad to see the last of something in his life.

III The Climber

During the six days and nights that Walter Bonatti and Cosimo Zapelli were hooked to the nearly vertical, ice-covered north wall of the 13,879-foot Grandes Jorasses above Chamonix, people in that mountain village and others talked of little else. They watched the winter sky nervously, worried about each approaching cloud. They muttered among themselves.

They all knew Bonatti. They considered him nearly superhuman, probably the strongest mountain man of all time, and the most obsessed. None had ever heard of Zapelli. To them Zapelli was an instrument Bonatti was using to force the mountain to its knees.

The people of Chamonix know and love the mountains. They understand the challenge of the high peaks, the lure of summit snow blazing like jewelry under the white sun. But they don't understand Bonatti. All the time he was up there they worried about him and cursed him.

"It is not courage, it is folly," they said, "not sport, but

80

fanaticism." When he conquered the mountain on January 30, 1963, they were neither surprised nor happy. They were simply relieved.

Zapelli, twenty-seven, is a doctor just out of medical school, and a close friend of Bonatti's. Zapelli had climbed before. He is brave and very strong, but in both bravery and strength Bonatti obscures him. In the mountains Bonatti obscures everyone.

Bonatti is thirty-two. He used to be a metalworker in a factory near Milan. He worked nights, and when the dawn came up he rode his motorcycle up into the Dolomites and climbed all day. Then, as now, he could get by on almost no sleep. At sixteen he went off in the night alone to bring down a party of lost and frantic climbers. At seventeen he scaled the Furggen in winter, the first time this had ever been done.

He was the youngest member of the Italian expedition to K2, in the Himalayas, in the early fifties. K2 is the world's second-highest mountain. Bonatti and a Hunzi carried all the gear up to the highest camp so that two older men could reach the peak the next day.

Caught in storm on the way down, Bonatti and the Hunzi spent the night in the open at more than 27,000 feet, without any gear, without even a tent. The Hunzi was frozen nearly stiff. Bonatti kept him alive all night, and in the morning got him down again.

In 1955, Bonatti climbed the needle-shaped Aiguille du Dru, near Chamonix, alone. It took him six days. For five nights he hung in a sack from a piton hammered into the vertical wall, getting what sleep he could.

The loneliness nearly destroyed him, he said. "I knew fear such as I have never known it." The wall he climbed is now known as the Bonatti spur.

He kept making "impossible" climbs year after year. In 1961 he was taking a client up the Freney Pillar. They met another group. A storm came up. Bonatti took over leadership of the entire group, seven men in all.

For six days the storm beat at them. Three men died. A fourth went mad. Bonatti brought his client and one other man

81

down with him. "Without Bonatti," the other two attested, "none of us would have got back."

One of these men went back up with Bonatti to make the first climb of the Petites Jorasses.

Now with Zapelli, Bonatti has done the Grandes Jorasses, too. At night the temperature on Bonatti's pocket thermometer went down to 31 below zero, Fahrenheit, and stuck there. Yet at times Bonatti climbed without gloves for a better grip.

By day Bonatti drove pitons into the wall, dragged Zapelli up, then climbed down to hammer the pitons loose so they could be used again higher up. By night the two men hung in sacks from pitons, dangling over the black void.

Bonatti estimates they got five hours' sleep in six days. On the seventh day, early, they reached the summit, then slogged down the other side in waist-deep snow. Reaching a road, they flagged down a car and got home to Courmayeur. It was then 6 P.M. Bonatti stayed awake till 6 A.M., gossiping about the climb with pals.

There is a popular misconception that such fantastic stamina and bravery are worth nothing commercially. This is part of the reason some mountain people condemned Bonatti's exploit in advance.

But Bonatti had sold the rights to his story to the Italian magazine *Epoca* in advance. Also, through his exploits he is so famous in the Alps that every tourist wants to climb with him. He cannot charge more than set tariffs for climbs, but he works more than other guides, sells more gear, and receives on occasion big tips from rich clients.

It may or may not impress him that mountains now bear his name. But it is clear that he loves them, especially the "impossible" ones, and is compelled by something inside himself to assault them again and again.

9

Fast Cars and Wrong Circles

THE WORLD OF MOTOR SPORTS

IN Europe, car racing (and to a lesser extent motorcycle racing) is the most serious sport. Scientific genius, money, national pride, and exquisite personal risk are all in it in equal amounts. At each Grand Prix or major sports car race, the investment by the nation, the factory, the organizer and the driver is tremendous. In American oval track racing in the past the machines were slapped together by mechanics. They were skilled mechanics, but still just mechanics. The nation had no stake in the matter, nor did even a major factory. The organizer had no great task, for an oval is easy to sell tickets to, and easy to police. The drivers still risked their lives, but only as individuals, not as standard-bearers; they were, except to a few devotees, nameless, faceless men. Dead today, forgotten tomorrow.

In Europe, at its simplest, a Belgian contract driver for an Italian factory wins, say, the British Grand Prize. At its most tragic, the Spanish driver of a German machine hurtles off the road to slaughter French spectators, and the entire continent goes into mourning. But the next year, almost certainly, the race will be run again. It is a showcase for the nation's industry, genius, and brave young men, and must not be allowed to lapse.

1 Fast Cars

In France, guys and girls—and hundreds of tired business men, too—flock to the 132 Go-Kart tracks that now litter the country. They seek a little fun and relaxation at speed.

And in England, a traffic officer observes that fans returning to London after motor races at Silverstone "seem to think they are all Stirling Moss. You get people doing 100 to 130 miles an hour on the M-1 Highway." The points to be made are that France's 132d Kart track will not be her last; and that the English traffic officer, E. S. Turton, is nonetheless against speed limits on public highways. Highways don't have limits in England, anyway.

"I think that how a man drives a car is his own business," says Turton.

All this may be incomprehensible to the American mind, conditioned as it is to rigidly controlled traffic, severely limited speeds, and huge comfortable cars that can easily seat four abreast and are so softly sprung they could cross a golf course at forty miles an hour without jostling a passenger.

In the United States, there is a minority that has discovered the sports car, and an even smaller group that has begun to be interested in Karting.

But the mass of the population persists in considering sports car owners as eccentric, and devotees of speed in any form as sick.

Indeed, speed is seen as an outlet for a titanic inferiority complex.

The one explanation that apparently has not been considered in America is the one that all of Europe long ago accepted as true: Men drive fast because it is fun. France's 132 Kart tracks have all been built in the last year or two. It is impossible to suppose that every Frenchman who frequents them is sick.

America pioneered the fat, comfortable car, which heels so drastically in a turn that the driver glides sideways in the seat and has no notion whatsoever how much tire adhesion he has left or how near the car is to flipping or skidding off the road.

In fairness to Detroit, all of Europe is gradually coming to this same type of machine. Comfort is on the ascendancy in Europe. Most of the new cars are more comfortable and thus less sporty than the old ones.

Formerly, however, the European car was small, tightly sprung, and equipped with bucket seats. It couldn't do more than sixty miles an hour flat out. No one was afraid of it and there was no publicity campaign, such as the American "Speed Kills" to worry the country.

The European car did not heel in tight bends. The driver did not slide across the seat in turns because the bucket seat held him fast.

Stirling Moss, generally regarded as the fastest race driver of the world, has said of racing cars, "I love the way they hold me."

But Dauphines, Volkswagens, Fiats—everything held a man in the old days. In a turn that the driver had entered a bit too fast, the car did not heel or skid. The tail sort of skittered in short jumps, two or three of them, outwards, in what racing drivers call "oversteer." This was accompanied by a slight squeal of tires and pressure on the driver's back and hips from the seat. If he accelerated, the skittering stopped.

It was fun.

If it sounds dangerous to drivers of American cars, this is because such sensations cannot be had safely in a big, soft Detroit machine. They can't be had in many of the big new European cars, either.

Not only are the tightly sprung cars disappearing here, but so are the winding roads (as new highways are built) on which it used to be so much fun to drive them.

This is perhaps the reason Karting is becoming so popular. Karts are tiny four-wheeled platforms powered by motorcycle or lawn mower engines. A Kart holds a man so he can feel— and enjoy— frustrating centrifugal forces.

As for highway driving, speed limits were not necessary

here when few cars could exceed sixty. They are becoming more necessary now and, in fact, do exist on some roads during some periods.

Most traffic officials, Turton among them, want to hold off speed limits as long as possible. Turton stations two or three times as many police cars along the M-1 after motor races than normal. This "sobers" drivers, he says.

He and most of his colleagues, however, don't believe in arbitrary limits, nor that speed kills, in itself. They do believe that driving a car is sport, or can be, and that drivers should be smart enough to watch their mirrors and to adjust their speeds to the conditions and circumstances of the moment.

Europe agrees with this thinking, and nearly everyone drives as fast as seems safe at all times, slides around bends whenever possible, and often refuses to let other cars pass until their drivers prove conclusively over several kilometers that they are faster.

In Europe the automobile is still regarded primarily as a contraption built for sport. It is romantic, glamorous. Sports car and Grand Prix races draw enormous crowds. Annually there are a quarter of a million people at Le Mans and the Nürburgring for races. The Grand Prix de Monaco draws more than 50,000, two and a half times the population of the place. In many countries the results of car races are not even printed on the sports pages of newspapers; they go on the front page, or on a news page, together with accounts of riding to hounds, horse shows, and other aristocratic pursuits.

There are also an enormous number of rallies which can be entered by anyone in any type of car. Basically, a rally is run in several stages of prescribed distances at prescribed speeds. A driver may neither undershoot nor overshoot his average without losing points. Points are also lost for dented fenders, for failure to get tanks sealed and route cards stamped at various controls, for not having correct licenses and/or passports, or for getting lost. The rule book for a rally may be forty pages long in complicated legal language; the winner is never known for at least twelve hours after the finish, and sometimes not for days. But Europe loves rallies too. Some draw 125 entries, some over 300.

In the capitals of Europe automobile shows draw tremendous crowds. Hundreds of perfectly ordinary cars are displayed, nothing more, but the public rushes to swarm around them. Newspapers devote pages and pages of space, prime ministers make official visits lasting an hour or more, and in the city itself hotels are filled and it is difficult to find a table at choice restaurants. Rome during the Olympics was not nearly so crowded as Paris (or Geneva, Turin, London) during the annual automobile show.

Cars have raced on public roads in Europe since 1894. The men who drove them were and are heroes to be talked about in hushed tones. Only in the last few years has possession of a car been within reach of the average European. Previously his only contact was in watching races or reading about them. In Europe the automobile has an exotic aura about it which has not existed in the United States for decades.

PORTFOLIO 2

LAMENT FOR A VANISHED FORM— SPORTS CAR RACING

These were the big open sports cars of the past. They could touch 180 miles per hour on the straight; they were raced nearly always on the open road by tough, daring professionals; they thrilled vast crowds, and they sold cars. The starts could be made singly, as (above) in Sicily's Targa Florio, the cars going off at one-minute intervals . . .

or the drivers could sprint across the track
to their cars, as at **Le Mans**.

The cars were pure racers, stripped of everything except speed and power. The races went on and on, hour after hour, while the world of car racing held its breath.

These are the two most successful sports car drivers of all time.
Olivier Gendebien, 38, a Belgian . . .

and Phil Hill, 35, from Santa Monica, California. With Gendebien he won
Le Mans and Sebring three times each, plus many other great races.

Each pit stop was frantic. Mechanics pounded off wheels and hurled others on in their place. Gas was poured, a tired driver jumped out, and a fresh one jumped in.

A Ferrari howls through the quiet Sicilian countryside. This scene was typical in the past. But alas, pure racing sports cars cost too much; they have been almost entirely replaced by showroom models, mostly two-door closed coupés, which factories produce in great number and are more willing to sponsor.

In the past a series of six or more grueling races determined the factory world championship each year. Now some of these races no longer exist; others continue, but much watered down. There is no more factory world championship for sports cars. Gendebien says he has retired, and Hill may retire, too. Only rarely photographed Enzo Ferrari (above), of the great marques, still produces the racing sports car.

MORE COMMENTS ON **LAMENT FOR A LOST FORM—
SPORTS CAR RACING**

1. The Targa Florio starts just after dawn, 40 miles east of Palermo, Italy, close to the sea front. The circuit is about 45 miles around. Inland it climbs into the mountains, rising to 2,000 feet. It rushes through villages, forests, meadows, the road potholed and twisting so violently that an average speed of 60 miles per hour is usually enough to win.

2. The Le Mans race is almost twice as fast. Each year, the winner averages nearly 120 miles per hour. And the race lasts more than twice as long: twenty-four hours, to a maximum of eleven for the Targa.

3. The Le Mans sprint is short, but decisive. Either you get your machine out fast or you are caught in a traffic jam of slower cars.

4. Gendebien never made much of a success of Grand Prix racing. No one knows why. But in sports cars his record speaks for itself. He could coax a wounded car on forever. He left the frenzied driving to others. He was calm. He made no mistakes.

5. Hill won the drivers' world championship in Grand Prix racing in 1961, but only in sports cars was he really at home. They suited his temperament. He could sprint when he had to, or hold back, or nurse his engine. He had the rare ability to be extremely careful at 130 or more miles an hour. In the very long sports car races this pays off more than any other skill.

6. Each two hours or so sports car races are interrupted for pit stops. Here a tired Dan Gurney jumped out and a fresh driver, Gendebien, is seen jumping in.

7. Tony Brooks's Ferrari in the Targa Florio.

8. Enzo Ferrari, now 65 years old, is rarely seen in public and almost never leaves Modena, Italy, seat of his tiny, but very exclusive automotive empire. His factory produces about 600 showroom cars a year, each selling for over $10,000. His customers are the rich, the elegant, the famous of the world, but he does not care about these people. He cares only about the perfection of the racing automobile. He is an arrogant, capricious man. He never goes to races. He orders his teams about by telephone. Engineers, team managers, drivers do what he says . . . or else. The Ferrari cars, ever more nearly perfect, go on winning.

II Motorcyclists Move Fast, but in the Wrong Circles

Racing motorcycles are nearly as fast as race cars; they are louder, scarier, and more spectacular to watch. Yet socially, the gulf between cars and cycles is unbridgable.

Race car drivers move in all the best circles of Europe, are invited to premières and meet kings and queens on nearly equal terms. It is definitely "in" to drive race cars. It is just as definitely "out" to race motorcycles.

Why this should be true is difficult to say, but it has always been so. Perhaps in the beginning of the age of the internal combustion engine, when Europe still teemed with nobility, it was observed that the duke (and especially the duchess) could move with dignity from point A to point B in a horseless carriage.

On a motorcycle, dignity was plainly impossible. If the duchess attempted to ride side saddle, she would, over the rutted dirt roads of the day, get thrown off. It was astride or nothing.

Perhaps a duchess or two tried it. If so, she got covered with dust and her posterior ached for days.

So motorcycles became something that a guy from the tough quarter of town drove because he couldn't afford a car. His girl rode behind him—astride.

Meanwhile, car racing advanced as the sport of aristocrats. The duke himself raced—if he had nerve enough.

Between the wars, such famous racing drivers as Bernd Rosemeyer, Tazio Nuvolari and Rudi Caracciola all started on the bikes, and not a single drop of noble blood flowed in their veins.

Today, motorcycle racing has it own Grand Prix tour consisting of about eight races in as many countries. A world champion is designated in each of four categories on the basis of points won in these races.

Some factories sponsor teams of racers and there is starting money for the stars entering each race as well as prize money for the winners. The amounts, however, are considerably less than in equivalent car races.

For instance, at Pau, where both race, the winning motorcycle earns $110, the winning car $500. Similarly, tickets to the three motorcycle races on Sunday cost less than half as much as tickets to the one auto race the next day.

Motorcycle races look frightfully dangerous. On fast turns, racers lean over so far that sometimes their exhaust pipes scrape the road and sparks fly. This is called "ear 'oling," the idea being to get your "ear 'ole" as close to the road as possible.

The biggest bikes (the 500-c.c. category) are not quite so fast as Grand Prix cars on the straight, but being much narrower, they can corner faster. Thus they lap a circuit nearly as fast as a car.

The fastest circuit in Europe is Spa-Francorchamps in Belgium. Grand Prix cars lap this at an average speed of 134 miles an hour, motorcycles at 125.

Motorcycles are more spectacular and look more dangerous because the laws of physics are so shockingly visible. When a motorcycle is heeled over on a 45-degree angle in a turn, a spectator can actually see the effect of speed and is terribly aware of what will happen if the rider loses control. In car racing, the physical forces are masked.

Motorcycle racers are not often killed, however. All wear a leather suit (pliable horse leather, usually) which is padded in strategic places. When bikes collide or skid off the road, the racer usually goes to the road rolling and sliding. This absorbs the shock. The leather suit protects him from the worst of the road burns.

A car racer, on the other hand, usually is hurled out of his car. Nothing absorbs the shock as he flies through the air. He smacks into things with terrible force.

No motorcycle meeting is complete without a sidecar race. The sidecars are more platforms than conventional passenger carriers. The sidecar rider must clamber about frantically to put maximum weight where it is needed, in each turn.

He leans way out, overhanging the road in some turns. He climbs up behind the driver in others. On the straight, he simply lies down flat with his legs hanging out the back.

Some look like they're praying, something for which no sane observer could blame them.

Here is an example of an accident in a motorcycle race.

There was once a famous English rider named Wal Handley. One afternoon at the Monthléry circuit near Paris, Handley had won a series of sprints and his tires were thin as he lined up for the final race. He had no spares.

He had had such good luck that day that he decided to ignore the thin tires. He got a fine start and was in the lead again when a tire blew out as he was passing the grandstand at great speed.

In motorcycle racing the thing to do is to jump off the bike once control is lost. If a man jumps off he usually will bound and slide along on the seat of his leather suit, dissipating speed and getting off with minor injuries.

So Handley, his bike slewing down the track, jumped off. Instead of landing on his backside, however, Handley had the bad luck to land on his feet.

He went striding across the track, about ten yards to the stride, through a fence, through the packed crowd, fetched up against a bar under the grandstand and said groggily: "I'll have Scotch, please."

10

"Deserving" Workers

THE WORLD OF SPORT
BEHIND THE IRON CURTAIN

BEHIND the Iron Curtain, sport is less like Western Europe with accent on exploit, more like the United States. There is no car racing and little mountaineering, no motorcycle racing and no bullfighting, of course. There is relatively little blood. The Party Line is against risk of life in sport; the Party Line is for team games because team spirit is a valuable national commodity. Soccer is very big behind the Iron Curtain, and ice hockey is enormous. Rugby exists, but is frowned on because rugby players break bones, which slows production at the factories. In America it is believed that sport is subsidized in the Communist countries solely for propaganda purposes, but this is nonsense. Sport is subsidized as an outlet for the emotions of oppressed peoples. If you let people scream loudly enough at enough splendid soccer, gymnastic or hockey teams, they will have that much less energy for screaming under the windows of politicians. If you come up with a Valeri Brumel breaking world high jump records every other week, so much the better. But the important thing is to use up the mob's lung power as harmlessly as possible. Entertainment behind the Iron Curtain (sports, music, ballet) is nearly always superb, and always the tickets

103

are cheap (or even given away), transportation is organized and the promotion beautifully sold. Thus even a swimming meet in Leipzig (the 1962 European championships), conducted day after day outdoors in pouring rain, is sold out, day after day, by soaked fans who cheer themselves hoarse.

I Czechoslovakia

The night the World Hockey Tournament ended in Prague a gala was given in honor of players and officials. The entertainment was superb—a gypsy orchestra from Bohemia, peasant singers and dancers in traditional costume, a mixed glee club from the Czech Army, and even a symphony orchestra.

But then the speeches began, most of them political. Again and again, Czech dignitaries insisted that hockey and other international sports were a means to peace among nations.

This is true, and the speeches were in bad taste only because none of what was said needed to be said.

When the speeches were over a buffet supper was served. Sologubov, the Soviet captain, moved from group to group shaking hands, throwing his arms around players from other countries. Lacking a common language, they could communicate in no other way.

A pair of American players, a Russian and a Czech ate together, grinning at each other, pointing at the food from time to time and saying, "Good, good." It was apparently the only word that all of them understood, except for "hockey."

They had all shared something—the heat and glory of combat. It had been a grand experience and they wanted to prolong it, and so they stood around trying to make conversation with smiles and gestures.

It is strange that a game such as hockey should promote good will among the players. For days these young men had been smashing savagely at each other. Tempers had become frayed. There had been tripping, mauling, slashing, and worse. It is strange but true that when you bash a man over

104

the head with a hockey stick in the heat of competition he becomes your friend for life.

Czech fans are surely the most vocal in the world, especially when supporting their own teams. They were equally vociferous in behalf of the hapless Finns, but they supported the Swedes only against the Russians.

In hockey the Czechs hate the Swedes. Before the Russians entered hockey in 1946 the two were the powers in Europe, and rivalry between them was intense. So it came as a surprise to hear a Czech crowd cheering for the Swedes.

All spectators were "deserving" workers who were permitted to buy hockey tickets as a prize for good work. But some were more deserving than others and had been organized into a pro-Russian cheering section. Every time this group, numbering about two hundred, attempted to cheer the Russians, a thunderous pro-Swedish roar drowned it out.

This may have had some political significance or it may have been nothing more than resentment at the way the Russians mauled the Czechs three days before. During the Russia-Canada and the Russia-United States games the crowd hollered about as loudly for one side as for the other.

But according to some who watched the games on television, the noise of Czech fans razzing Russian players in the Czech-Russia game was so loud and prolonged that TV officials began manipulating the volume control so that cheers and boos came out at about the same level on home sets.

It was not necessary to see a game or hear the roar of the crowd to know that hockey was a religion in Prague. A stroll down Prikopy Street, a turn around Wenceslaus Square was enough.

The hockey motif was in most of the shop windows. Flashy ties dangled from clutched hockey gauntlets. Elaborate pyramids of pucks vied for attention with stacks of sausages. Photos of rugged body-checking stood in counterpoint to a variety of ladies' bonnets.

In the window of a dress shop a gown hung draped over a

pair of crossed hockey sticks. It was a type of gown that went out of fashion in the West some years ago, but the sticks were new, polished, and of the latest mode.

Outside newspaper offices people stood reading posted reports of the games. In windows along the street there were giant placards with the scores of previous games. Before each window there were people, some just gazing, others discussing the merits of this or that player.

It was cold and gloomy, the temperature below freezing. Clouds hung low and cold all day, trapping the coal smoke which rises from the buildings and imparting an acrid bite to the chill air.

It was not pleasant to be abroad as night fell, but still the crowds stood there. Hockey was on everyone's mind.

That was fine with the Czech authorities, who promoted the world championship tournament with the verve of Madison Avenue. Sixty of the biggest stores were induced to compete via window displays for special prizes.

Even the elegant Moser Crystal Company was among the competitors. On tall, exquisitely fine vases, castles and crests used to be engraved. But during tournament week some of the designs were of crouched goalies and onrushing wings.

It was no accident, either, that preliminary rounds were held in outlying cities like Brno and Bratislava. That way, deserving workers in factories all over the country could buy tickets to at least one game.

Others could watch games on factory television sets. Non-factory workers, doctors for instance, could obtain tickets through hospitals. In all cases government functionaries handled the tickets and only the "deserving" were permitted to buy them.

The 180 foreign journalists who went to Prague for the championships were deluged by brochures and booklets purporting to show not only the astonishing variety of the Czech sporting program, but also the enthusiastic acceptance of that program by all the Czech people.

There was, for instance, the story about the two men on their way to the High Tatra Mountains for a trade-union-sponsored winter holiday.

One of them stared morosely out of the train window.

"This is my first visit to the mountains," he said. "My mates in the factory told me I would enjoy it. So they gave me a holiday voucher for my good work and here I am."

"What am I going to do there?" asked the second man, who was equally glum. He was nonathletic and elderly. "I've got no outfit for winter sport. I don't know how to ski. And I don't like hiking. I am used to sitting there at my desk and playing about with figures." He addressed the others who shared their compartment. "Do any of you play cards or chess?"

"Don't fear, friends," a man across from them boomed heartily. "I also went for such a holiday for the first time last winter. I had the same fears. But these were soon dispelled when I was able to borrow everything that I did not possess. Skiing boots, sticks, and so on. What I didn't know about it they taught me."

The story has a happy ending, of course. For both non-skiers the week in the mountains "passed like lightning." The two friends who had approached their vacation with foreboding met again in the railroad station.

"How was it?"

"Wonderful! Next time I'll go gladly."

"I wholeheartedly agree."

The story ends with some figures. About 90,000 persons spend a week in the mountains every year on trade-union-sponsored winter holidays, paying only 70 crowns (about $5) to do so. It is to be hoped that some of them are there because they want to be, not merely because they had the misfortune to win holiday vouchers at the factory.

The key word in all Czechoslovakian sports probably is factory. Soccer is the nation's number one sport, and all of the teams represent one factory or another. The players are supposed to be workers first, soccer stars second, and it is claimed that there is no such thing as a professional athlete.

Brisk trading of players between factories used to be practiced, nonetheless. Say the Skoda Automobile Works needs a new inside right. Its choice may be one Miroslav Novak of Dynamo Prague. Novak currently is only an assistant foreman at the plant, so Skoda offers him a job as supervisor, with corresponding increases in pay. Novak decides to switch factories—and teams.

However, steps are being taken to wipe out this decadent practice and it is not so common now as it was a few years ago.

Organization of players begins long before they are old enough to work in factories. Presently there are 60,000 juvenile soccer players and 30,000 juniors. More than 30,000 boys play hockey in various leagues. Over 100,000 boys and girls, some of them as young as ten, take part in skiing competitions.

The mountains of eastern Czechoslovakia rise to about 8,000 feet, are beautiful, but are relatively unencumbered by lifts. These youngsters must hike to the top of every slope they want to ski down.

Everything is organized in Czechoslovakia. Methodical physical training of boys and girls in the most important branches of sport began on a large scale in 1948. Since then there have been competitions of every imaginable kind, including such capitalistic favorites as figure skating.

There are tournaments in volley ball, table tennis, rowing, parachute jumping, girls' basketball, and gymnastics. One of the most popular sports is cross-country motorcycle racing. Cross-country means just that. Roads are not used. The machines roar across plowed fields, ford streams, climb hills, zig-zag through forests.

Ordinary citizens can leave the country only with the greatest of difficulty, but Czech athletes are among the most widely traveled in the world. In 1962 the national soccer team even toured South America.

The biggest single Czech sporting event is the National

108

Spartakiade, a two-week exhibition of mass gymnastics exercises. About 400,000 persons take part and something over 2,500,000 look on, filling a 100,000-capacity stadium twice a day, every day.

To a Westerner it does not sound like a thrilling show, but it is perfectly in keeping with the announced purpose of the Czech sporting program: "The people's democratic social system comprehensively supports the application of the principles of socialist physical training in practice."

II East Germany

In sports as in all else Germany is divided.

East Germany has been done over in the Soviet mold. There is no longer any such thing as a professional athlete there. Boxers and bike racers are amateurs. So are soccer and basketball teams, which are composed of factory workers, policemen, or soldiers. These teams play in organized leagues and some are very good indeed.

There is no contact between the East German leagues and their counterparts in West Germany. However "friendship" matches between individual teams were often played on a home-and-home basis before the wall went up in Berlin.

The center of East German sports probably is Leipzig, which has a new 100,000-capacity stadium—the ninth largest in the world—and is the seat of the German Physical Training College, which confers academic degrees and whose express purpose is to train teachers of sports. At present there are about 150 teachers and about 800 students in the college.

There are eight training halls in judo, weight-lifting, wrestling, fencing, gymnastics and the like, a swimming pool with seats for 10,000 spectators and outdoor playing fields.

East Germany has marvelous skiing in the mountains near the Czech frontier. These resorts are much admired, even by West Germans, and they have produced the only two ski jumpers who can compete on equal terms with the Finns and Norwegians.

East Germany has produced the world amateur bike racing champion, Gustav Schur. In the canoe and kayak racing world slalom championships, individual and team victories often fall to East Germans.

The propaganda values of sport are never overlooked behind the Iron Curtain. The exchange programs of all the Communist nations are in full flower in East Germany. Foreign teams, coaches, and students are constantly invited there, with a slight accent on visitors from the Orient, the Middle East and Africa.

In contrast to East Berlin's role in the East German sports program is the isolation of West Berlin. The city has many amateur teams but they do not compete in West German leagues because they are too far away.

Regular trips to West German stadiums would be expensive—the nearest of them is one hundred fifty miles away and a team could not defray expenses by playing other matches on the way. Trips would have to be made by air because many teams include refugees from East Germany who would be seized if the team tried to cross East German territory by car or bus.

Lacking topflight teams of its own, West Berlin supports instead touring attractions from the free world. The Harlem Globetrotters play there as do Jack Kramer's professional tennis troupe, wrestlers, and bike racers.

The 1936 Olympic installation and the Avus motor racing circuit are in West Berlin and both escaped the bombing. The Avus has at least one meeting a year and the Olympic stadium often stages major track meets.

At most of these events twenty per cent of the tickets used to be reserved for East Germans who were invited to come over and be entertained. These tickets were paid for in East German marks on a one-to-one basis although normally it took nearly five East marks to buy one West mark. This policy was subsidized by the West German Government. The wall put a stop to this.

East and West Germans compete as one team only in the

Olympics. The Olympic Committee remains the one world organization that has ordered the Germans to get together or else, and has made it stick.

III Bulgaria

In Sofia, Bulgaria, the fifth parachute world championships were held in a state-fair-type atmosphere. About 70,000 persons milled about exhibits, stands, and merry-go-rounds. Music and commercials blared from loud-speakers. There were pavilions where people dined or danced.

Occasionally, almost incidentally, a plane sailed over and someone jumped out of it. The grounds were quite a way out of town and it was difficult to get there. Bulgaria has little private transportation and not enough trolleys and buses to handle the crush.

Army trucks were pressed into service, shuttling back and forth from the city crammed with happy people.

The show had been briskly pushed by the government. Posters and placards were stuck to nearly every lamppost in the city. Newspapers had hammered away for weeks. There were flags, bunting and blaring loud-speakers all over. A fifty per cent reduction in railroad fare helped bring in thousands of peasants from the country.

Entertainment-starved Bulgaria was delighted with the show.

IV Poland

Sport in Poland is a bulky governmental machine with the Glowny Komitet Kultury Fizycnej i Turystyki (the Main Committee for Physical Culture and Tourism) on top and the individual sports federations on the bottom. For instance, the Polish Track and Field Federation can invite foreign teams only after receiving permission and funds from the G.K.K.-F. T. During the 1961 visit of the American team, gloomy weather on Saturday and torrential rain on Sunday cut the total crowd by 100,000 and receipts by a corresponding amount.

These receipts would have been turned over to the G.K.K.-F. T. in any case, but the Track Federation still comes out the loser. The Track Federation must fight each year for a share of the government's sports budget.

If it can show huge profits on meets like this one, it will, of course, receive more money for its program. If it can't, the Fencing Federation or the Volley Ball Federation may receive more money next year and the Track Federation less.

In Poland, the G.K.K.F.T. also supervises the sports lotteries, sports museums, factories that manufacture sports gear and something called the Scientific Institute of Physical Culture.

The country's biggest stadium in Warsaw seats 100,000 persons. There are stadiums in Western Europe that hold more persons, but none with as many seats. Most Western stadiums have no seats in the end zones. They are reserved for packing standees in, chest to back.

Soccer is the number one sport in Poland. The leagues are composed of army teams, police teams, and sports clubs. In the lower leagues, there are university teams, too.

The sports clubs recruit players from the mines and factories. The teams are "amateur." If a miner is a dazzling inside right, however, he may work in the mine only three months a year.

The rest of the time he receives his pay while on "leave" to the soccer team. It is the same for other athletes. However, there is no trading of players.

The Poles love soccer, but they are not very good at it these days, though the national team did beat Russia in May, 1961, by 1–0. That game erupted into a riot after the Polish goalie was fouled, apparently accidently, by a Russian.

An ambulance rolled onto the field to carry the goalie off. The outraged screaming and whistling of 100,000 Polish fans was deafening. Men heaved bottles onto the field and launched furled umbrellas like javelins. When the game ended, a mob ambushed exiting Russian players and beat up some of them.

Some arrests were made and a trial of sorts the next day sent many men to jail for three months. Worse, fans were threatened with no more international matches in any sport. In the way of entertainment not much else exists in Poland besides sport and Polish crowds have behaved mildly ever since.

Soviet teams, unpopular in Poland, will come to fence and be beaten, but never to box or run and be beaten. Individual Russians or club teams have boxed or raced here, but never a national team.

There is cross-country motorcycle racing in Poland, some auto rallies, much hunting and fishing and some hiking.

Hitchhiking has become something of a sport. The government has encouraged it as a means of enabling the young to travel to vacation areas.

Booklets of tickets are sold to the youngsters. Each time the hitchhiker is picked up by a motorist, he gives the man a ticket. At the end of the year a new car is awarded to the motorist who has collected the greatest number of tickets.

The Lodz soccer team won the championship of Poland one year. In a delirium of enthusiasm the directors of the team promptly ordered brand-new motorcycles for every player.

But when the bill arrived—the players by this time were driving around proudly on their new cycles—the directors found to their chagrin that there was not enough money in the treasury to pay.

Then someone came up with a brilliant idea. At least it seemed brilliant at the time. Why not print 500,000 post cards with the team picture on the back? Fans would snap them up in a matter of hours.

The disinterest of the fans in this idea was simply amazing. No one wanted the cards. In addition to owing money for the

113

motorcycles, the directors now owed the printer for the cards.

Then someone got a second idea. Why not make the purchase of the cards mandatory? Each time a fan tried to buy a ticket to a game, just sock him an extra zloty for a post card. Soon the cards would be gone, the motorcycles would be paid for, and the directors would be off the hook.

The first result of this second brilliant idea was riots in front of the ticket windows. Then, possibly because the players were now spending more time driving girls around on their new cycles than practicing, the team commenced to lose one match after another.

With this the riots in front of the ticket window gradually ended, replaced by a general boycott of the team altogether.

Receipts of the Lodz team fell off day by day. The motorcycles still have not been paid for and the better part of half a million post cards remain to be sold. The directors are waiting anxiously for someone to come up with another brilliant idea.

V Hungary

For Laszlo Papp, middleweight prizefighter, winner of Olympic gold medals for Hungary in 1948, 1952, and 1956, the end may be near.

For at the age of thirty-six, his thighs are thickening. His belly is as flat and hard as strenuous training can make it, but there is a layer of puffiness over it. His punch no longer knocks opponents down. He has had more than 300 fights, only twenty of them professional. He turned pro five years ago, receiving the necessary special permission from the state to do so. Papp said he wanted to win, if not the world middleweight championship, then at least the championship of Europe. Hungary gave him her blessing.

Of his twenty professional fights he has won eighteen and drawn two. The two draws were atrocious home town decisions. In Milan he beat an Italian eight rounds to two on the cards of every ringside scorer except the official one.

Reports of this fight described the crowd as stunned by the verdict. Papp smiled enigmatically beneath his pencil-thin mustache and quietly left the ring. He is a quiet man, but he says he won't fight again in Italy. His twentieth fight was in May, 1962. He beat a Dane in Vienna, to win the European Championship.

Papp has had a long career. All things considered, it has been as successful as that of any other boxer. He began fighting the year the war ended, a longshoreman who preferred using his fists to unloading river steamers. He fought during all those desolate years. Bigger and bigger crowds went to watch him. His flat-footed punching style was widely admired; perhaps he and it typify the Hungarian people.

Papp is stocky, wide-shouldered, with thick arms and thighs. His hair is curly, his nose straight and fine, his face unmarked. He has worn his mustache for many years.

By 1956, when he won his third Olympic gold medal, he was a hero in Hungary of the magnitude of Y. A. Tittle or Mickey Mantle.

Governmental permission to turn pro and fight for money in the West was unparalleled. So was the movie he made. It was called "Heavy Gloves" and was based loosely on his own life. Aimed at the juvenile audience, it extolled virtues such as hard work, honor, love of family.

These virtues are part of Papp's character. Asked what he likes in life, he replies: "What is mine. My wife, my son, my mother, my home."

What does he hate?

"Lies, baseness."

He is a religious man. He would not miss Mass on Sunday. When he comes to Paris to fight, he always visits the Cathedral of Notre Dame.

He says he wants to fight three more years at least, but one wonders if he can last that long. Whether he can or not, his future seems assured.

The Hungarian Government long ago awarded him a plot of land on which to build a house. He has a well-paying government job. In Hungary, hardly anybody owns a car. Laszlo Papp, national hero, does.

Once, someone asked him if he was interested in fighting in the United States.

"What for?" he replied, "I'm not hungry for money. A man can eat steak only once a day."

But certainly he would prefer training in Paris to training in Budapest, someone said.

"I like Paris very much," Papp said. "It's nice to be back here. But do you know something? People think a lot of me in Hungary. I have a good life there."

VI The Soviet Union

"In the Soviet Union we have some totalizator betting at tracks, but no bookmakers," said Professor Vladimir Vite, the foremost Soviet harness racing authority.

"But it is not the betting which counts with us. It is the horse. The perfection of trotting stock. In time, as human nature changes, we feel that betting will die out completely." Professor Vite is a tall, elderly man with round spectacles perched on a long thin nose, and aluminum teeth that flash like cutlery as he speaks. His manners are courtly and his knowledge of American trotting encyclopedic.

Now he switched from his interpreter and attempted to explain himself in a mixture of halting English and halting French.

"We have had 100,000 crowds at tracks where there was no betting. Of course there were other races too, like boys on horseback chasing girls on horseback."

"Naturally everyone is rooting for the boys," murmured Lewis Burton, the vice-president of Yonkers Raceway, "in order to discover what happens next."

What the professor was attempting to describe was state-fair-type harness racing, which exists on a large scale in the Soviet Union.

No one is sure how good the best Soviet trotters may be.

116

Professor Vite was in Paris with two steeds that were to trot in the Prix de France at Vincennes. He remarked that these two were not the best Soviet trotters, merely representative ones, thereby discounting poor performances in advance. The two nags did very badly. He also told tales of a pure white Arabian stallion whose name is Bravi. According to Professor Vite, the animal stands seventeen hands high (a hand higher than the great Jamin) and can trot a mile faster than any Western horse, Jamin included. But Bravi couldn't make the trip. He is at stud this time of year.

No one in the West has seen Bravi to this day, and he may be a myth.

All Russian horses are state-owned and -trained, under the Ministry of Agriculture.

Valeri Brumel left Paris for Moscow, having stopped for thirty-six hours to see the sights. He was on his way home after having trounced John Thomas, officially the world's best high jumper, in three straight meets in New York.

Brumel's stopover was significant. Not long ago Soviet athletes had no time for sightseeing. They were never let out alone. As recently as the 1956 Winter Olympics they weren't even lodged near other athletes. They would meet interviewers only in groups or after careful screening.

They were different from the others.

Brumel's trip to Paris was in many ways the final collapse of Soviet isolationism in sport.

It appears that the stopover was, first of all, in the nature of a reward because Brumel and Igor Ter-Ovanesyan, the broad jumper, had done so well in New York.

It appears also that the Soviet Embassy in Paris received word of their visit at the last moment.

There is no way of telling what the Embassy's reactions would have been in the old days. But its reaction now was atypical. It telephoned the Paris papers to tell them that Brumel was in town. The Embassy and all Russians were very proud of eighteen-year-old Valeri.

117

The Embassy didn't even know where Brumel was—probably at Versailles, the Eiffel Tower, or one of those places, it said.

Reporters from *l'Equipe,* the Paris daily sporting newspaper, raced to Versailles and several other spots, but finally found Brumel gazing up at the towers of the Notre Dame Cathedral.

Brumel and his companions were asked how they had liked America. The answer came from Leonid Khomenkov, the head of the Soviet delegation.

"The crowds at Madison Square Garden were marvelous to us," he said. "In three track meets Brumel became, I think, the most popular athlete in America. Ter-Ovanesyan got his share of the applause too."

Standing before the Cathedral, Brumel seemed surprised that anyone was interested in him. He seemed extremely modest and a little shy. He explained his victories over Thomas by saying: "I think I was in a little better shape than he was. I must catch up on the practices I missed while in the United States in order to be in the best possible shape the next time I meet Thomas."

Brumel was asked whether there was bad feeling between Thomas and himself.

"Well, said Brumel, "he wasn't smiling after that last defeat. But surely I wouldn't have been either if the results had been reversed. John Thomas is very correct."

So is Valeri Brumel, despite his youth. As a parting question, *l'Equipe's* reporter asked him to name the pleasantest memory of his voyage.

The boy answered promptly (and gallantly): "The joy of having discovered your marvelous Paris."

So are they all correct, all the Russians. They have the reputation in Europe of being marvelous sportsmen. They play the game according to the rules. They win gracefully, they lose honorably. They obey the officials. They rarely, if ever, whine.

This was seen again when the 1961 Russian hockey team,

conceded by nearly everyone to be the strongest the Soviet Union ever had sent to a world hockey tournament, was defeated, 6–4, by the weakest Czech team seen in the West in many years.

The skilled, powerful, disciplined Russians may have figured they had this 1961 tournament already won. So the Czechs clambered all over them, pressured them, unsettled them, and beat them.

It must have been a galling defeat, particularly when the victorious Czechs heaved gloves and sticks into the air, kissed and hugged one another and somersaulted over the ice in paroxysms of joy.

While this was going on, the Russian team stood at attention at the blue line, waiting to listen to the Czech anthem, waiting to salute the victors. Because the happy Czechs couldn't contain themselves, couldn't form their own line, the Russians had to wait a long time.

They waited, chins up, staring straight ahead though many another team would not have. One wanted to applaud them.

Victory is important to the Russians, make no mistake. But it is impossible to watch them often, in many sports, without being convinced that playing correctly is important too.

11

Bring Money

THE WORLD OF SPORT
ON THE RIVIERA

BEHIND the Iron Curtain sport seems gray; on the Riviera
it is tinted rose or mauve, like the colors in the Mediterranean
when the sun goes down. I lived a long time in Nice, and
there is much sport there to report, most of it luxurious, full
of color, beauty, and money. Then you go a few miles inland,
where the peasants hunt wild boars with mongrel dogs and
shotguns. The Riviera is a good place to see both sides. It
is also the opposite side of the world from the countries of
the East.

I King-size Golf

If a golfer stands on the seventh tee of the Monte
Carlo Golf Club and peers cautiously over the edge, he can
see almost all of Monaco—2,500 feet straight down.

From such a height the city looks toy-sized, its Casino too
tiny for drama, its horse-shoe-shaped harbor filled with
yachts whose spars bristle no thicker than matchsticks. So far
below, the Mediterranean seems docile as a swimming pool.

The seventh hole—and its awesome view—is calculated to
weed out golfers suffering from vertigo, and also those who

120

cannot control a tendency to slice. A ball sliced wickedly enough could wind up bouncing down the streets of the principality, a few minutes later.

The Monte Carlo golf course, set on a mountainside, is one of the most unusual in the world. It presents spectacular views, fascinating golfing problems, and a glamorous clientele. Most of all, it is unusual because it exists where neither a golf course nor patch of grass has any right to exist. Terrain such as this interests only goats—and golfers.

Along the Riviera the mountains go right down to the sea. The soil is stony enough at sea level. Higher up there is no soil at all. The Monte Carlo golf course was built more than fifty years ago amid the rocks and gorse atop the mountain that rises behind the city. It was begun in 1909 and was built entirely by hand.

An army of men moved down what were to be fairways, smashing boulders with sledge hammers. Behind them moved women with baskets on their backs, gathering the broken rock and carrying it to the edge of the scrub forest. When the boulders were gone, earth was carried up on the backs of a few mules and many men.

Some of the earth came from as far away as Italy. It was graded by hand. In some places terraces had to be contrived to keep it from washing away. The grass that was sowed came from Britain and America. A spring was found that produced just enough water to keep greens and tees from burning out during the hot, rainless summer.

In a year and a half the work was done. The course was opened by the kingly gamblers and the gambling kings who inhabited Monte Carlo at the time. Naturally they did not pay to play. The course was owned by the Casino and hasn't changed hands. The object of the links was to keep heavy plungers happy during those hours when there was no action at the tables.

Nowadays anybody can play the course. Plungers and kings still play for nothing. For others there is a greens fee of $3. Clubs and caddies can be hired. Many of the latter are sturdy

121

peasant women from neighboring villages who hike over to earn a few francs during their spare time. The nearest of the villages is Peïlle, nearly an hour and a half away by foot.

Among recent players have been Baudouin, King of the Belgians, who shoots in the low 70's, ex-King Michael of Rumania and pretenders galore. The King of Sweden was a frequent visitor, as was Prince Pierre, the father of Rainier. Rainier does not play.

Aly Khan used to play the course often, sometimes bringing Rita Hayworth with him. Among the film stars who have broken 80 here are Bing Crosby, Bob Hope, and Clark Gable. Gable is said to have socked the ball harder and straighter than any of them.

Naturally those people were not asked to pay. The criterion in celebrity-conscious Monte Carlo seems to be that nobodies must pay $3. But if you are rich enough to buy the clubhouse they will make you an honorary member and you can play for nothing.

This course has never been popular with pros, and there never has been a major international tournament here. There are two reasons—it is too short (just under 5,000 yards) and too tricky. With some fairways terraced and some greens set on the edge of precipices there is too much premium on luck.

As the club steward, Aldo Amari, puts it: "A good player can always defend himself out there. A bad player . . ." His voice trails off and he shrugs.

Par is 67. There are seven par-3 holes and two that are rated as par 5's though they are only 430 and 417 yards long respectively.

The most striking hole is the fourth, a 260-yarder. The tee is 130 feet—the height of a thirteen-story building—above green level. To the right is a road, to the left a bizarre rock formation that thrusts high up beside the narrow fairway and resembles Roman ruins.

Because there are only thirty to forty players a day, the course is in beautiful condition. Wild berry bushes, cork oaks, maritime pines and cypress line the fairways. In the fall the grass is green, the leaves on the trees have the autumn colors and there is a breath-taking view of the snow-peaked Alps far beyond the back nine. There can be few more invigorating rounds of golf anywhere.

II The Underwater Hunt

In English it's called skin diving. But the French, who claim to have invented the sport on the Riviera just before World War II, certainly named it more aptly. They call it *"La Chasse Sous-Marine"*—The Underwater Hunt.

The hunt began with masks made of inner tubes, and home-made spears. Only a handful of enthusiasts had the courage to go down wearing such apparatus.

But those few found Greek galleys that crumbled at the touch, anchors lost by Barbary pirates, and antique cannon encrusted with coral and nearly swallowed by the bottom of the sea. They discovered luridly colored cliffs that began many fathoms deep and disappeared into the darkness even farther down than that. They found caves to explore, and hills and valleys, all far below the surface and never before seen by man. The names they tagged these discoveries with were as lurid as the undersea colors—"Dragon's Bay" and "Valley of the Dead" for instance.

When they went fishing they managed to jab their flimsy spears into vicious conger eels four or more feet long, into manta rays and merou, the Mediterranean rock bass.

Sometimes the merou weighed one hundred pounds. Perhaps the spear was primitive, but the fish had never been hunted so deep, and so allowed a man to swim close.

All through the war these enthusiasts spread the gospel. And the war itself spurred the development of frogman-type gear that could easily be adapted to civilian use afterward.

In 1946 a man named Henri Broussard founded the Club Alpin Sous-Marin. By 1949 he had two hundred members paying dues of about $10 a year. He now has nearly 4,000 members in various categories.

Other clubs sprang up in Juan-les-Pins, Nice, Monte Carlo, and Menton. Soon they stretched from Marseilles to the Italian border. More and more gear was produced. It, and the sport itself, was exported to the United States.

The sport had no birth pangs. The Mediterranean itself breathed life into it. Who could resist the sea's exotic secrets, the lure of sunken galleys, grotesque rock formations, and merou a hundred years old? No other sea on earth could exert such pull.

But of growing pangs the sport had—and has—plenty. First the fish grew wary. It is now extremely difficult to get a shot at anything bigger than, say, the flat, gold-flecked sar, a fish unlikely to weigh more than a pound or two.

Next, the commercial fisherman began to complain about the invading army of divers. A law was passed prohibiting spear-fishing with the aid of air bottles in the coastal waters of France. The spear fishermen had driven the big fish deep. By this ordinance they were forbidden to go down after them except off the most distant islands—Corsica and Sardinia, for instance. One of the effects of this law has been to divide the sport into two categories—fishing and exploration.

With bottles strapped to their backs the explorers go deep and stay down nearly half an hour. Their excitement is intense, for who knows what they may discover on the bottom of the sea. The fishermen are limited to short plunges in which they hold their breaths as fiercely as their guns.

And thirdly, La Chasse Sous-Marine has grown terribly dangerous. The danger is not from fish, although conger eels, rays, and occasional sharks can be fatal companions.

The danger is from man himself—from his insatiable lust to go deeper and deeper—and from the refined equipment that permits him to do so. Plunges thirty meters deep without bottles now are commonplace in the Mediterranean and so is death.

The type of tourists that the various Riviera clubs will take fishing or exploring for half a day for $6, all equipment included, are relatively safe. The tourists are supervised, and they go only as deep as the pains in their ears will let them.

But the skilled diver can go as deep as a six-story building is tall, thanks to a new type of mask that is form-fitted around the nose. When the pain hits the ears at depth, the diver now can squeeze his nostrils, which equalizes the air pressure inside his skull. The pain disappears and he is able to go down and down and down. As he nears the bottom he is thrilled by the strangeness and wonder of it. It is so beautiful he forgets about coming up. He grows lightheaded, still swimming down.

Because of the new mask, thirty young men or more die in the depths of the Mediterranean each summer.

III Bring Money

"Summer vacation? Why not cruise in comfort and luxury aboard a 142-ton motor yacht; two double and two single staterooms, two bathrooms, large saloon and dining room, secluded sundeck; Fiat car, speedboat for water skiing, charter inclusive."

In various corners of Europe and the United States ads like this one appear each spring. They have several things in common. Few are gauche enough to include so commercial an item as price; the name of the yacht is rarely, if ever, given; but in all cases interested parties are advised to direct themselves to the Riviera city of Cannes, which modestly believes itself to be the pleasure-boat capital of the world.

Nowhere else, so it is claimed on the Riviera, are so many boats stuffed into such tiny and picturesque harbors. Nowhere else are there so many varieties for rent or sale. Nowhere else are there so many romantic places to sail them to. Nowhere else is sunshine so nearly guaranteed and the scenery so spectacular.

Why not cruise to Corsica, Sardinia, Majorca; or round Italy and make for Venice, the rocky inlets of Yugoslavia, or Greece? Why not indeed? All it takes is a few thousand dollars.

The oldest and most respected Riviera agency is André

Glémot and Company, whose office fronts the harbor at Cannes. Glémot has 158 available yachts in his files. The cheapest of them rents for $5,000 a month, not including food for the crew ($2 per man per day) or fuel (25 cents a gallon; average consumption perhaps five gallons an hour). Such a boat would displace fifteen tons, and be sailed by a two-man crew.

The most expensive would displace more than 400 tons, have a ten-man crew, burn more than twenty gallons an hour and cost $20,000 a month to rent.

"I don't think that's too expensive, do you?" asks Glémot in a mild voice. "In any case, from May to October we don't have enough boats. They are all taken."

By whom? By "ordinary people," according to Glémot. He mentions only four celebrities with whom he has done business—Rita Hayworth, the late Errol Flynn, and Elizabeth Taylor and Eddie Fisher. The latter pair once hired the *Olnico*, 203 tons, seven-man crew. Price, $15,000 a month.

A yacht agency is in an excellent spot to chart a kind of social graph, according to Glémot, whose clients are American, English, Dutch, French and Italian, in almost equal proportion. But he notes that now for the first time since the war there are beginning to be many Germans, too.

Before the war a single wealthy man chartered a yacht. Now yachts are often hired by five or more couples who share expenses. That way "it doesn't cost much more than a month in a first-class hotel would cost," explains Glémot, "and they have freedom, they can cruise around."

A yacht agent is also aware of the tax structure in all countries. If the names and prices of yachts are rarely given in ads, it is because income tax men watch such ads carefully, ready to pounce. The Briton who can rent his yacht to an American in France for a trip to Greece, usually feels he need not declare his profit back home. In this regard he can rely on the complete discretion of a man such as Glémot.

A yacht agent is also hounded by a type of European journalist searching for the scandals that sometimes erupt on yachts. With the advent of left-wing and Communist papers even scandals are sometimes not necessary.

For instance, one British reporter prowls the Cannes harbor regularly. Recently he spied a well-known British society woman frying her own breakfast eggs on deck on board her yacht. The yacht, he reported, was worth £35,000, but Lady So-and-So was down to her last shilling and could not afford a cook.

Neither Lady So-and-So nor her set regarded this report as funny.

The major agencies along the Riviera waterfront refuse to handle boats not big enough to need a crew. There is too much risk that something will happen to the boat, and not enough profit. Riviera yachting is fun, but bring money.

IV Wild Boar Hunt

Between the wild boar and the domestic pig there is a distant family relationship and they have the same long, flat-tipped snout. But where the pig is gross and moves meekly to be slaughtered, the boar is sleek, long-legged and afraid of nothing.

The wild boar is brown or black. He may be four feet from nose to tail and weigh more than two hundred pounds. He can outrun a dog and kill a man. He is the most dangerous and, consequently, the most sought after game in the Mediterranean part of the world.

He is hunted by men who know what they are doing, and he is a fearsome sight to the unarmed. He will attack anything, particularly farmers who get in his way when he is running from hunters.

One recent week boars attacked two French farmers, Jean Bouleau near Dorat and André Lievens near Vincourt. Bouleau, fifty-five years old, was struck down as if by a bull, the boar tearing at his leg. In its fury to destroy, the boar had forgotten the hunters beating noisily toward it, and now one ran up and shot it dead. Bouleau was rushed to hospital.

127

Lievens was tilling his fields when the boar rushed out of the forest straight at him. The boar evidently had been hunted before and had mistaken the cries of farm workers for hunters beating the bush.

Straight at Lievens it charged. The farmer grabbed a pitchfork, and as the beast rushed in, planted the five teeth of the fork in its throat. The handle snapped off and the boar didn't even slow down. M. Lievens leaped onto a cart and grabbed another fork. The boar kept leaping, and the farmer stabbing, until finally the boar died.

The boar weighed 180 pounds. All that day Lieven's friends and relatives came by to view the carcass and to congratulate the farmer on his lucky escape.

The beasts are hunted in the Black Forest by what is left of the German aristocracy, and in the mountains of Yugoslavia by Marshal Tito and his friends. One receives the impression that only bluebloods qualify for a shot at a boar.

This is not true, for wild boar is also the favorite game of peasants in every corner of Europe. In groups of ten or more they hunt it with shotguns and mongrel dogs they have trained themselves. The danger adds spice to their hard, drab lives. They love the sport of the chase through the clear cold air of the mountains where boar are found. And they love the taste of the meat itself. Boar meat does not taste like pork but has a gamey, wild taste that somewhat resembles venison.

On the slopes of the Basses Alpes (Lower Alps) just behind the Riviera a "battue" is organized nearly every Sunday from September 1, when the season opens, until snow covers the valleys, about December 1. Day by day the peasants can watch autumn advance, and the snow line moving down the mountains. When the snow reaches the valley floors boar may no longer be hunted legally; their tracks are too easy to find in the snow and there is danger of the race dying out.

A "battue" resembles a classic tiger hunt. The group splits up. Half a dozen men, shotguns loaded with heavy shot, take up posts on trails boars are known to travel. Another half

128

dozen with dogs go around the back of the mountain, then beat noisily toward the waiting hunters.

Boar like it best where the underbrush is thickset. They are difficult to find because they roam so much, searching for the roots and acorns they eat. They may cover thirty miles in a day. The hunters may find tracks only a few hours old, but the boar that made them may already be miles away.

Boar do not run from the dogs, but from the noise. They do not fear dogs. If brought to bay by a pack, a boar will kill them one at a time, slashing upward with the tusklike fangs that protrude from its lower jaw. Once wounded by a boar, a dog will never hunt them again.

The hunt may last an hour, or all day. If a boar is shot it is cut up on the spot, one portion going to each man. Men who furnish dogs get an extra share. The meat is then hung for eight days, after which it is roasted, usually on a spit over an open fire.

The peasants who live in the Lower Alps are mostly wood-cutters. Some keep flocks of sheep or goats. They live in old stone farmhouses. Some have electricity now; none has plumbing and the only heat is the roaring fire in the main room. Dirt roads lead in there, and these are snowed-in half of each year.

They do not know much of comfort, these people, but they know beauty, snow-peaked mountains and lower slopes glorious with the colors of the autumn hunting season. And they certainly eat well, at least when feasting on roast boar.

V Dead Pigeons

In many places, shooting at live pigeons has been replaced by the shooting of clay ones, or skeet. This is cheaper and it provokes no outcry from the humane societies.

But at Monte Carlo, and at a few other elegant stations such as Vichy, Deauville, and San Remo, live pigeons are still blasted out of the sky by a few professionals, who make a tidy living via prize money and side bets, and many of the idle

129

rich of Europe.

Undeniably, the shooting of live pigeons has an aristocratic appeal to it, a feeling of waste and luxury. This is particularly true when the pigeons are provided by the Monte Carlo Casino, flutter briefly above the Mediterranean, quiver in a hail of buckshot, then plummet into the sea.

The season at Monte Carlo lasts from January 28 to March 14 and is said to be the longest in Europe. In that period an average of one hundred and fifty shooters a day compete for about $150,000 in prize money. Pigeon shooting is self-supporting; the prize money comes from entry fees, which may be $60 for a single one-day competition. Pigeon shooting at Monte Carlo is an expensive sport.

Every day for six weeks there is a different competition. Each has a fancy name such as Prix de Paris or Prix de Rome. Prize money ranges from $1,000 for the Prix d'Encouragement to $9,000 for the Grand Criterium of Monte Carlo.

The size of the entry fee depends upon the prize money at stake. It costs only $12, for instance, to enter the Prix d'Encouragement, but $60 to enter the $6,000 Grand Prix de Monte Carlo. For this money the competitor is assured of only one shot. If he misses, he is through. If he hits the pigeon, he is permitted to shoot another when his turn comes again.

After a dozen rounds the one hundred fifty entries have been trimmed to perhaps ten. Now the pressure builds up. With so few shooters remaining, a man has just enough time between shots to get terribly nervous. It is late in the afternoon. The light is failing. Furthermore, he is shooting so often that his shoulder begins to hurt from the recoil of the 12-gauge shotgun.

As his next turn approaches, a man thinks of the money at stake. His heart is thumping. The bird flies up. The man shoots nervously, and misses. He is out.

One recent weekend, the Grand Prix de Monaco was won by Dr. Angelo Moccia, a portly Italian physician. From a distance of about eighty-eight feet, he killed twenty-five

130

pigeons with twenty-five shots. Two men who missed after getting twelve straight birds shared tenth place.

Sometimes two men duel into the darkness blasting one pigeon after another without a miss. When it is too dark to see, they stop. The contest is resumed the next morning. Some competitions are all over after fifteen rounds. Others last thirty or forty.

Either way, five hundred pigeons a day are killed, or about 25,000 during the season. They are raised in Spain and brought in each day by air. Pigeon shooting is a big sport in Spain.

Entry fees for a week's shooting come to about $200 per shooter. This money pays the gun-cleaners, locker-room boys, waiters, pigeon keepers and the cost of the pigeons themselves, in addition to the prize money. The Casino gives the dead pigeons to its staff members, who eat them or sell them. The Casino makes no profit on the pigeon shooting but it presents a ticket for its aristocratic private gambling rooms to each aristocratic shooter. All in all, the Casino does not make out too badly.

The shooting takes place on a ledge below and behind the Casino facing the Mediterranean. Five collapsible metal boxes fan out about sixty-five to ninety-eight feet away, depending upon the competition, from where the shooter stands.

When the shooter cries "pull," an attendant presses a button that collapses one of the boxes. A ball rolls off the top, startling the pigeon. The bird takes off. Bang.

Most pigeons are dead before they are five feet from the box. All have had their tail feathers removed. This makes them fly up erratically, but also slowly. If they are not hit, most of them manage to gain altitude and fly away. The tail feathers will grow back in time.

A few fail to gain altitude, stop beating their wings after a while, glide into the sea and drown. There are always some poor fishermen waiting there in boats. Monte Carlo pigeons are considered tasty.

A glass-enclosed room at a corner of the range is crowded

131

with gamblers who bet on each shot. Many shooters gamble, too, betting for or against opponents while awaiting their own turn.

The clubhouse is elegant. It's similar to a golf club, with restaurant, bar, lockers, and gunroom. On the walls are marble plaques bearing the names of big winners since 1872, which is when men first started to shoot pigeons at Monte Carlo.

12

Ups and Downs

THE WORLD OF BIKE RACES

T HERE are people who claim that bike racing is dying and perhaps it is. Fewer Europeans ride bikes every year, and increasing traffic is forcing the races off highways on to back roads where fewer people watch.

But to Europe, bike racing is still the most grueling sport, the most dramatic, the most glorious. There is so much suffering in it, so much courage and strength, so much effort, so much of the scenery it pedals through and over, that it is still the supreme sport, the supreme spectacle, the supreme test of athletic might. Across the mountains await money, fame, rest for aching legs. But first the riders must sweat the big drops.

Bicycle racers begin training in February on the roads and mountains of the sunny Riviera. Soon they are pedaling 120 or more miles a day.

Their bodies become flat, sinewy, and hard. Their arms and legs, exposed to the sun, turn the color of caramel. The rest of them stays the color of aspirin.

The first half dozen city-to-city races are held on the Riviera. They are usually won by rookies who disappear when the older hands start bearing down.

Then the great road races begin. The first is Paris-Nice,

which whirls South at 25 miles an hour followed by an ambulance load of racers too sick or injured to continue. The finishers travel 900 miles in nine days, sprinting across the plains, struggling up mountains.

It is a brutal race, but an easy one compared to those that follow: the Tour of Italy, the Tour of Spain and the twenty-two-day, 2,700-mile Tour of France.

These races leave a trail of broken bikes and broken men. Bicycle racing is no game played on lush lawns, lasting only an hour or two. An average day's leg is seven hours—150 or more miles of uninterrupted pedaling.

The racers go day after day without rest, eating badly, too tired at night to sleep properly. They collapse from exhaustion, from sunstroke.

They wobble groggily to the top of mountains and sail down them at 60 miles an hour, trusting to the rush of wind to revive them. Sometimes it doesn't, and when the road turns they crash.

Bicycle racing in Europe is one of the bloodiest, most physically punishing businesses in the world. The bikes are fragile. Made of aluminum, they weigh only seven pounds and their tires are as narrow as a man's thumb. At high speeds they are difficult to control. A break in the pavement, a patch of sand or oil, a too-sharp turn—all spell disaster.

Each year in each major road race half a dozen or more ankles, shoulders, and skulls are fractured. Fatal accidents are infrequent, but they do happen. Racers have gone over cliffs, have crashed into walls and trees head first.

There are collisions, too. Some road races have a hundred or more entrants, a dense pack jockeying away from the starting line each morning. The racers are deft, but inevitably comes the morning when one bike nicks another. Both go down—and so do twenty more bikes behind them.

Road surfaces are of concrete, gravel (which will tear a fallen racer's shoulders and hips to the bone), and tar hot enough from the sun to scald a man who tumbles down wearing only shorts and thin shirt.

134

Cobblestone streets in medieval villages are even worse. Laid centuries ago, they are made slick as ice by rain. The heavy stone blocks are spaced just enough to grab the wheel of a speeding bike and wrench it out of control—sending the racer flying over the handlebars.

Even those who do not crash suffer intensely, from saddle-sores, from colic, from the side effects of drugs which all racers take when so near total exhaustion that they cannot continue without a stimulant.

It is a grim, grueling business, but each year hundreds of young hopefuls clamor for a place on one team or another. Some are accepted, not as potential winners, but as "dome-stiques." Every star is accompanied by domestiques. He uses them as windbreaks, he appropriates their bikes when his own breaks or has a flat, he sends them to box in or harry other stars.

There is no glory for domestiques and only an insignificant amount of prize money. The disillusionment of most of these youngesters is cruel. Some hang around for years, hoping for a break, a chance to show the speed which had made them champions of their village. For most, the chance never comes.

Stars do not come up through the ranks. Usually they start on indoor tracks racing against the clock, perhaps setting new world records for miles an hour, like Jacques Anquetil. When Anquetil finally began road racing it was as team leader, not as domestique. He won the 1957 Tour de France, his first season on the road.

Nearly every year there is a new star coming up, starting as team leader, earning (in starting money, prize money, endorsements, contracts with commercial sponsors of road races) $100,000 or more a season.

He brings his records and titles with him: world pursuit champion, world record holder for miles pedaled in an hour. He is young, confident, and already famous.

But what will he do on the road, the experts want to know? What will he do when he has crashed a few times, when the sun burns down, when the road is slick in the rain?

135

What will he do when the mountains loom ahead and there are still a thousand miles to go?

There is only one word for the Tour de France. That word is enormous.

Everything about the Tour is big. To get an idea of its length, imagine a bike race that starts in San Francisco, winds down through the Rockies across the deserts into Mexico, out across Texas and back through Nevada to San Francisco. That's about 2,700 miles in all—120 racers straddling saddles as narrow and hard as a greyhound's snout, legs pumping the thin, frail bikes all the way.

The caravan that accompanies the Tour is big. It includes publicity vans, trick motor scooter acts and trucks blaring commercials. More than thirty miles long, it begins passing a given point ninety minutes before the racers and passes continuously at twenty-five miles per hour until the first racer is in sight far down the road.

With something like 15,000,000 fans lining the roads, the publicity caravan has an audience greater than any national magazine or television broadcast.

One sporting paper has twenty-three reporters assigned and devotes five pages a day to its coverage. A normal provincial daily like the *Nice Matin* awards the Tour one complete page out of fourteen.

Communist papers like *Le Patriote* give fifty per cent more space than that, evidently aiming for new readers among Tour fans. On a typical morning *Le Patriote* has seven by-lined stories on the Tour, taking up the entire back page and half of page one.

The Tour is so gigantic that borders can not slow it nor common law halt it. This goes for every vehicle in it and there are more than 350 cars, trucks, and motorcycles in addition to the bikes.

It sails through Luxembourg without showing a passport and cuts through a corner of Belgium at top speed with the border guards cheering as loudly as anyone.

136

One Saturday, near Valenciennes, France, a Tour vehicle skidded in the rain and slid broadside into the crowd. A dozen persons were injured and one man's leg was broken.

The car occupants—race officials—got out, looked over the damage, left their names with the police and then drove on hurriedly.

All concerned understood that this car had its place to keep up in the caravan and that nothing must be permitted to interfere with the Tour.

In a few minutes the bikes began to flash by, a swirl of spokes and color. Even the injured stopped moaning and leaned forward for a better look.

At the top of the pass 3,000 people wait to cheer the bicyclists of the Tour de France. The sun is on the jagged peaks all round, but the pass is 7,000 feet high and it is cold and windy. Although it is mid-July, most fans are wearing coats.

The road to the pass has been closed since noon. To get there the crowd had to go up in the early morning. For many hours it has been waiting with mounting excitement. It is nearly three o'clock before someone spies the first of the bikes, still far below, climbing painfully, slowly. A shout goes up in French:

"Ils arrivent!" Here they come!

Up and up the fragile bikes pedal. Now they are close enough for fans to see the colors of the jerseys—blue, orange, crimson, violet, gold—and to pick out the favorites.

The scores of riders are strung out a long way down the mountain and even the leaders pass very slowly. They have been climbing for sixteen miles, the road getting steeper all the time. The gradient is now 17 degrees. Cars would be in first gear here.

The riders are nearly exhausted. Sweat pours off them and the strain of the climb pulls at their faces. They are close enough to touch.

The crowd cries out to its favorites, "Pump, pump."

Gendarmes hold back the crowd, but a few persons break

137

through and run alongside, pouring bottles of water over riders. Some riders give a grateful nod; others are too tired even for that. They keep pedaling.

At the summit, hands thrust newspapers forward. Riders grab them, spread them under their jerseys as a windbreak for the 60-mile-an-hour run down the mountain. It will be fifteen or more miles before they pedal again. Sweat will dry. They will be cold and stiff when they reach the bottom.

A few miles farther on, the climb will start again, together with the suffering. The flat stages of the Tour are interesting, but the Tour is won and lost in the mountains where few spectators watch, where no one can help, where a man is alone with his bike and the climb. The mountains are where the danger is, too. Every year there are a few terrible accidents.

In an early stage of the 1960 Tour, Gastone Nencini of Italy and Roger Riviere of France sprinted fifteen minutes ahead of the pack, Riviere winning by inches. After that all knew that either Riviere or Nencini was the winner of the Tour. They were fifteen minutes ahead, and the two strongest men in the race anyway.

Nencini was considered the most daring rider in Europe at coming down mountains. Often he bragged that he could gain five minutes on any man in a twenty-mile downhill run. Nobody understood how he got round corners at such speed, but he did.

Now, coming out of the Pyrenees in 1960, Nencini was plunging down crouched low over his handlebars, sliding, skidding the corners, rarely braking, and Riviere just behind was trying desperately to stay with him. Nencini skidded in a corner, but recovered. Riviere skidded, did not recover, plunged through a retaining wall and crashed sixty-five feet down into a ravine.

Riviere lay there between two great boulders, his face in some wild flowers, his back broken in two places and thought: "No one saw me go over—they will all pass by; please God someone saw me."

A teammate, Louis Rostollon, did see him. Rostollon

sprang from his bike and started screaming: "Stop, stop. It's Roger, he's gone over the wall."

Men climbed down to him. "I think my back's broken," Riviere moaned. "I can't move my legs. Oh, don't touch me, don't touch me."

A helicopter got him out. He lived, but is still partially paralyzed and will never race again. He was twenty-five then and earning about $100,000 a year. He is still the world's record holder for miles pedaled in an hour.

The Italian, Nencini, went on to win the Tour. The following spring, rocketing down a mountain in Italy, he, too, crashed over a wall and down into a ravine. A patch was torn off his scalp, he was unconscious, and when they got him to a hospital it was found that his back was broken also. He is back racing again now, but not very fast any more. He hasn't won anything since his accident.

One year the Tour was won by Frederico Bahamontes of Spain, known as the Eagle of Toledo. When he went home there was a tumultuous parade and reception. The governor of the province made a speech, the mayor provided Bahamontes with enough land to build a house, the Cardinal sent his blessing and there were prayers of thanksgiving in the Cathedral. A sculptor was commissioned to commemorate the achievement; he carved a statue not of Bahamontes's face, but of his legs—the legs which had won the Tour de France.

Bahamontes went back to France to fulfill about fifty contracts for indoor appearances—at about $400 per contract. When he went home again this time, he was coaxed into fighting a bull in Toledo's arena. A tremendous crowd turned out, the bull sent the Eagle flying, but in the end Baha killed it and was granted both ears and the tail by his devoted and delighted fans.

But the next year Bahamontes quit the Tour on the second day, claiming to be sick. For eleven months he had reigned as the King of Europe, but now suddenly he was a bum again. No one believed he was sick. Disappointed coaches and journalists heaped abuse upon the Eagle, as did other riders.

He's sick mentally, they said, and they began to call him The Turtle from Toledo.

Bahamontes that season lived all the extremes that make up the life of a star rider. In the spring, when still the hero of Spain and Europe, he raced in the Tour of Levant, crashed coming down a mountain, and broke his leg.

From his hospital bed, the Eagle announced he would be fit in time to race the Tour of Spain, which was then six weeks away.

He did race it, too, but he was out of shape and was roundly booed by fans who had expected victory. Once Bahamontes got so angry he leaped off his bike and clobbered an insulting fan with his tire pump.

He was disqualified from the Tour of Spain. There was talk of suspending him for the season, but since he was the defending champion in the Tour de France and the leader of the Spanish team, nothing was done.

Bahamontes cannot stand being booed. When they booed him in France he got off his bike once more and announced: "Frederico, he is sick. Frederico, he cannot go on."

In shame and derision, he went back to Spain. Alejandro del Paz, the president of the Spanish Cycling Federation, said, "Bahamontes is going to be examined by a doctor. After that he is going to be examined by a psychiatrist. And if both their findings are negative he is going to suffer the consequences of what he has done."

In bike racing the peaks are high. And from them a rider can plunge a long way down.

Mr. Average European Bike Racer spends each July 10 pedaling across Provence in a pack of his fellows. He pedals easily this thirteenth day of the Tour de France because the country is flat. He gossips with his pals in the pack and eats constantly (a favorite recipe: orange juice mixed with rice). From time to time he figures out how much of the Tour's $110,000 he has won so far.

Unless he has crashed recently, he feels good. The road is

flat, the stage comparatively short (only 110 miles), the Alps are behind and the Pyrenees too far ahead to see. He still has 1,000 miles, nine days to go, but mostly he manages not to think about it.

Mr. Average Bike Racer at his peak is between twenty-seven and thirty-two years old and has a wife and children whom he rarely sees during the season. He is a big hero everywhere he pedals. There are girls after him, but mostly he is too tired.

He is about five feet seven inches tall, weighs about 140 pounds. He is thin and wiry, except for his thighs, which are enormous. There is a particularly bulging muscle on the inside of each thigh just above the knee.

His legs are shaved smooth as a girl's, and glisten in the sun from the substances his masseur has rubbed into them to keep the muscles from bunching up. The veins in his legs stand out like in the legs of a race horse.

Mr. Average Bike Racer smells of wintergreen oil in the morning as he pedals from his hotel through the streets of the town toward the starting line. When the day's stage is over he smells of wintergreen mixed with sweat.

His eyes are deep-set, his cheeks sunken, and his metabolism so abnormal that it borders on the freakish. His heart probably beats only about forty times a minute. Perhaps he was born that way. Perhaps it developed. But he can pedal swiftly over high mountain passes where the air is so thin that a non-bike racer would have trouble climbing a flight of stairs.

He eats and drinks constantly while pedaling, in order to keep his strength up: sandwiches, fruits, chickens, and two pounds of sugar mixed with just enough water to make a thick syrup.

Often he rides seven hours or more at a stretch. He cannot afford to stop and get off his bike, even to relieve himself, which he does while rolling.

He is not above snatching food and drink out of the hands of spectators, and he rarely bothers to thank people who offer him food or drink or throw water over him as he goes by. He flings bottles, chicken bones, and the like over his shoulder without regard for where they land.

He brags constantly about how good he is.

If he is good enough he may earn $100,000 or more a year. He will live in a fine house, buy a mink coat for his wife, buy a heavy insurance policy on himself against accidents while racing and spend four to five months every winter hunting, fishing, and bragging.

He crashes five or six times a year, at least once in his life seriously. His elbows, knees, and chin are covered with scars, and usually he pedals with fresh scabs and bandages somewhere on his body.

He won't win much after about thirty-four but can keep going on reputation until forty or more. His name will draw fans to velodromes; his name is worth plenty to the apéritif, television, or refrigerator company to whose team he belongs, and who pays him most of what he earns.

When he is old enough, he will look up at the Alps and Pyrenees he has pedaled over so often and wonder how he ever did it. This is what all of the nonracers who go with the Tour de France wonder every year.

Even when you see it being done it is incomprehensible. The principal emotion aroused by the Tour de France is awe.

THE

UP-AND-DOWN

WORLD

OF

BIKES

Riders wait at start
early each morning,
pretending to be
unaware of admirers.

Sometimes terrain is cobblestone back-country roads. . . .

Riders eat all the time to keep up strength.

They break down—
here racer
with flat tire
signals team car
for spare.

ey suffer from heat, thirst, saddle sores. Sea invites, but it is not for them.

In their colossal fatigue they often crash.

For the winner each day, there is glory . . .

And even kisses!

1. The scene is Grenoble during the 1961 Tour de France. That day, the bikes went over the Alps.

2. The 1962 Paris–Roubaix race. The cobblestone roads near the Belgian frontier are known as "L'Enfer du Nord," The Hell of the North.

3. Joseph Groussard of the French team, reaching for food in the Maritime Alps during the 1961 Tour de France.

4. Paris to Roubaix, 1962.

5. The beach at Nice during the 1961 Tour.

6. This is Henry Anglade of the French team after crashing in a tunnel in the Pyrenees during the 1960 Tour. Twenty-two other riders piled up on Anglade in the dank, dark tunnel. All remounted and rode on.

7. Kurt Gimmi of Switzerland wins a stage at Luchon, in the Pyrenees, during the 1960 Tour. The race that day had climbed over three passes, the highest at 7,000 feet.

8. Martin Van Geneugdegen of Belgium, the stage winner at Bordeaux during 1960 Tour, is bussed by Miss Bordeaux.

13

While Europe Cheers

THE WORLD OF EXHAUSTION

THERE are many degrees to exhaustion, and the degree which is most popular in Europe does not exist in America at all. This may be because nearly total exhaustion is difficult to make commercial. It takes too long to achieve, and you must entertain the crowd in some other way in the meantime. An American, having never seen very much exhaustion, is not interested in it; indeed he imagines it to be rather disgusting.

Total exhaustion is not pretty, but it is not disgusting either. There is a great deal of it in European sport, and the athlete who can still get the job done though his muscles tremble uncontrollably and his eyes are glazed by fatigue is considered the most admirable hero of all. The spectacle of bleary-eyed men pressing on day after day when every exhausted fiber of their bodies begs for a rest seems to be admired above all else by European fans.

I Exhaustion on Foot

From Strasbourg on the German frontier to Paris is 331 miles. That's about sixty minutes by airliner, eight

154

hours by car or three days and nights on foot, provided a man walks fast and does not bother about sleeping. This latter figure is not a theory but a fact based on actual experience.

Most years in the spring thirty determined individuals set out in shorts and shirts to hike to Paris nonstop. The race is organized by a Paris newspaper and the prize is a new car.

It seems a long walk just to get a free ride, but one man, Gilbert Roger, practically could go into the used-car business. He had won six times and was a heavy favorite in the most recent race.

Roger was forty-eight years old. All the fastest men in the race were old-timers, some of them over fifty. All agreed a man needed experience more than speed.

Younger men always hurried off in the beginning, only to find that the wall of sleep encountered the third night was too steep to scale. The old heads hung back and Roger was the best of them.

But this time Roger met his match, a thirty-nine-year-old factory worker named Edmund Guny. For three days and nights Guny plodded relentlessly on, stopping to rest, breathe, doze, soak his feet only ten minutes here and there—a total rest time of two hours, fifteen minutes.

His family took turns driving alongside of him—encouraging him, urging him to forget the colossal blisters on his two heels, his hunger and aching fatigue, urging him to keep walking.

A downpour the third night weakened Roger. Guny caught him twenty kilometers from the end and beat him to the tape by an hour. This is referred to in race jargon as winning with a sprint. The total elapsed time was seventy-one hours and forty-five minutes.

The exhausted Guny went to bed, there to dream about his new car and driving, not walking, back to Strasbourg.

Everybody cheered.

II Exhaustion on Wheels

The Le Mans car race lasts twenty-four straight hours. Two drivers switch off every two hours or so. This relieves incipient cramps perhaps, but is not nearly time enough to relax, to sleep. Round and round the cars go, all night at 115 miles per hour or more with tired men trying to hold their eyes open behind the wheel, trying to hold that absolute pitch of concentration which is a man's only security at such speeds, knowing in their fatigue that any error could be fatal.

The major bike races last three weeks or more, seven hours a day, day after day. Chafed backsides are only one of the riders' problems. Saddlesores erupt, and under constant chafing from the seats, infections start. Some harden to boils. Riders tie raw steaks to the seats, hoping it will help. It rarely does. Even the one-day races are more often tests of stamina than speed. One, Paris-Bordeaux, starts at 2:00 A.M. in the darkest part of the night, the riders pedaling for 350 miles, sixteen straight hours to reach Paris.

The Automobile Tour of France is an eight-day, 5,000-mile disguised Grand Prix. Each year a hundred or more cars start. Twenty-five or so finish, no one in them having slept more than catnaps in a week.

Three nights of the Tour are set aside for "repose," but neither drivers nor mechanics go to bed for more than a few hours. There is too much to do to make sure the cars are fit to roll the following dawn.

In theory the mechanics drive all night, leaving the drivers fresh to drive the hill climbs and closed-circuit races scheduled for the following day. But in fact they share even the night driving, for the next day the mechanic has to be awake enough to flash signals from the pits, to oversee hundreds of other details.

Each year there are those who manage to run out of gas in the middle of the night on some desolate back country road with no hope of being rescued till morning.

There are those who try to make up time by sailing through

predawn fog but end up ramming other cars which had been proceeding more prudently. There are crashes galore, more than twenty of them, usually.

One year on a single stage of the race, one man lost a wheel, another his wife (she said she had had enough of this nonsense and was going home), and a third lost all of his illusions together with his brakes while plunging down a precipitous mountainside.

But the saddest fate of all is that of the ten or so cars which fail the very last day with the finish in sight.

One driver recently was so tired that he lost control trying to enter a narrow bridge at about fifteen miles per hour. The car climbed slowly up the embankment and fell into the river, which at this time of year was only a few feet deep. The driver could not react fast enough to do anything about it. The next car also went out of control but stuck on top of the embankment. The two men in the river climbed up and helped push the car free so that it could reach the finish even if there was no further hope for victory.

In 1956, the year the Marquis de Portago won the Tour, it drew fourteen pro drivers of the front rank. Nowadays there are only two or three and the Tour attracts little international interest.

Most pro drivers say it is too much work and avoid it. It is loved only by those who consider exhaustion a pretty thing and simple ability to endure the most winning quality in sports.

A man named Pierre Marie, a garage mechanic from Rheims, France, recently returned from his two-week vacation. No loafer, Pierre. Instead of lying in the sun, he hopped on his motor scooter and drove to Jerusalem and back, a mere 7,000 miles in fifteen days.

The trip out took six days and ten hours. The scenery included Switzerland, Trieste, Salonika, Istanbul, the Syrian Desert, Damascus, and Amman as well as some Alps, part of the Balkan chain, and the Taurus Mountains of the Middle East

157

Coming back, Pierre, who is forty years old, attempted to go nonstop from Trieste to Rheims (more than 1,000 miles), but he collapsed from bounding up and down in his saddle, from lack of sleep, and lack of food. He finally had to stop at a hotel. Otherwise, he would have made the trip in only fourteen days.

In Rheims now, they are talking about submitting Pierre's performance as a world record. The only trouble is, no one knows whom to submit it to.

III Exhaustion Spanish-style

As final evidence of the European fan's fascination with exhaustion, take the case of Jaime Ostos at Toulouse. Ostos, then twenty-five years old, is a bullfighter, and that year was the second most active matador in Spain and southern France. He is an earnest, steady young man, but not a great star. If he fought often it was mostly because promoters used him to fill cards on which the top names—Antonio Ordonez and Luis Miguel Dominguin—were appearing.

In most of his fights, Ostos killed two of six bulls on the program, working about forty minutes. The work was, of course, dangerous. It was also exhausting, demanding constant movement and intense concentration.

At Toulouse there were six bulls, as usual. But this time there was only one matador—Ostos. He was going to try to play and kill all six himself. A second matador was standing by, just in case. But it was Ostos's show if he could do it.

One-man corridas have been tried before, though not often, and almost always with unhappy results. Dominguin himself had failed miserably eight years before in that same arena.

A two-hour corrida simply demands too much from the body and spirit of one man. Matadors have been known to faint from exhaustion, sometimes falling toward the horns in the process.

As the matador becomes more and more tired his morale sags to insupportable depths. No sooner is one bull dispatched

158

than a fresh one takes its place. As the afternoon drags on, each succeeding bull seems bigger, stronger, and wilder to the dazed man who must kill it.

Ostos's first triumph was to attract 8,000 persons to the arena. Dominguin had drawn only 5,000 eight years before.

These spectators had not come to see art because Ostos is not an artistic bullfighter. He is valiant and hard-working. His repertoire is moderate.

No, the crowd had come to see exhaustion, to watch a man suffer, to watch two kinds of courage. Fearlessness of the horns was expected of him. Did Ostos also have the kind of courage that can make a man go on and on when there is nothing left inside him but the will to do so?

With his first bull Ostos worked hard but killed badly, and the crowd hooted and whistled derisively. The second bull was small but strong. Ostos gave everything he had, burying his sword to the hilt at the end and winning both ears and the tail.

The third bull was apathetic. Ostos was competent but tired. The crowd was behind him now and gave both ears to him. The fourth beast was a hooker and unworkable. Ostos, leaden with fatigue, dispatched it at length. The crowd was silent.

The fifth bull was one of the biggest and wildest ever seen in Toulouse. The combat was a riot of danger and swirling color, the arena rocked by the noise of the crowd and the air electric with fear for the risks Ostos was taking.

Where Ostos got the strength, no one knew. On and on the fight went, pass after pass without a pause or a moment's respite from tension.

Finally the bull, mesmerized by the cloth and gasping for breath, broke off the fight and Ostos swooped in with the sword. The bull dropped like a stone.

The delirious crowd awarded two ears, the tail, and a hoof to the matador. Ostos, nearly unconscious on his feet, hung on the barrier, gasping and retching.

The last bull raced out. The crowd was roaring for more,

more, more. Ostos tried to give it, though now he had nothing left. Sometimes he tottered and nearly fell as the bull charged. Then, near collapse, he started to vomit. He hung two minutes gagging on the fence, then staggered back and killed the bull.

The crowd awarded one final ear, making the day's score seven ears, two tails and one hoof. The crowd carried the exhausted matador back to the hotel on its shoulders, his arms filled with flowers.

14

The Ideal Resort

A WORLD OF SKIING

As competition, skiing is completely unexciting to watch—there is no head-to-head racing, and it takes a clock calibrated to the hundredths of a second, a clock started and stopped by an electronic gadget, to discern the winner. Furthermore, the condition of the snow varies so greatly between the passage of the first skier and the last that a ski race isn't even really fair sport.

All this is compounded by the fact that in Europe so much is at stake in ski racing. The national tourist industries of the Alpine countries rise and fall in direct proportion to the success, or lack of success, of the national ski teams. Whichever country wins the most races next winter will draw the most money-spending, skiing tourists the winter after. Furthermore, for the skiers themselves, a few victories can mean a life of ease in later years. They can run ski shops or hotels, they can record songs or go into the movies.

There is much pressure in ski racing, much money invested in it and reaped from it. It can be exciting to photograph, but it is usually dull to watch and dull to read about.

But skiing down mountains for fun, your skis whispering over the snow, the wind against your face—ah, that is another thing altogether. . . .

Most skiers spend as much time reading travel brochures as they do actually skiing, and many can tell you how many lifts, how many miles of downhill runs exist at every major ski station in the Alps. They trade information among themselves, and plan winter vacations which in most cases never come off. All are searching for the ideal place to ski. Does it exist? None know for sure, but all hope so. All hope to be first to find it, too.

Where would the ideal ski resort be? Not in Vermont or New Hampshire, that's one sure thing. Skiing is a sport which excites the whole man. It makes him thirsty, hungry, alert to sights and sounds and smells. At the end of a day he can feel every muscle in his body. He feels incredibly alive. He is in the mood for the exotic. Vermont and New Hampshire have been called many things. They have never been called exotic.

So the ideal resort must be abroad: Kitzbühel, Zermatt, Cortina d'Ampezzo. One of those places. If you happen to live in "one of those places," it is, of course, no more exotic than the Catskills. But for our skier an Alpine resort would burst with strangeness—strange language, dress, habits, strange drinks to get unexpectedly high on. When not skiing there would be local color to sop up, gawk at, photograph, talk about. The comparatively cheap hotels would seem, to any skier nurtured in and around Big Bromley, unimaginably luxurious: fires in the hearth, breakfast in a warm bed, boots polished every time you left them outside your door. Service when you want it, and with a smile.

Our skier is young enough, not too rich yet and must leave home, ski and return within the airlines' seventeen-day-excursion-fare period. This means he can only spend a day, or part of a day, in whatever city the plane sets him down in. So the ideal resort must be close to a major airport, and that major airport must be an exciting city.

Most Swiss resorts are served by Geneva or Zurich, most French ones by Geneva, most Austrian and German ones by Munich.

162

None of these places is a bit exciting to me. Are they to anyone? Perhaps. But we can all agree that Venice is exciting, and Venice is the gateway to Cortina.

I once arrived in Venice at 6:00 A.M. after an all-night train ride. It was January, very dark, and the train up to Cortina would leave at nine. I checked my bag and skis at the station and then wandered through the town in the cold, damp dark, trying vaguely to find the Piazza San Marco without asking anyone. Although I knew how to say "Dov'è la Piazza San Marco?" I didn't quite dare to, for my uncertainty would disclose that I didn't speak Italian. By walking silently about the city I could be, for an hour, as Venetian as any man. No one would know I didn't belong. It could be my city too.

I walked along the canals, crossed the bridges, looked up at buildings bulking dark in the night. I felt awed to be there and I marveled at a city all around me which I sensed but could not see. Then Venice began to stir. A light came on behind shutters; a church bell tolled mournfully somewhere; a gondola went by, a soundless shadow in the water below. Men came out of buildings carrying lunch pails and walked along the canals to work. I walked with them until it began to get light. Then, in the gray dawn that was cold and damp, I walked back toward the station, stopping along the way to drink a coffee standing up in a bar filled with workingmen.

That afternoon as I skied at Cortina, it seemed to me that the world was incredibly big and good. The skiing cannot possibly have been as good as I remember it. To this day I have never seen the Piazza San Marco. I say this without regret.

Call Venice the doorway to the ideal resort, or else grow some mountains beside Rome, Athens, or Madrid. After that, the ideal resort should be so beautiful a man would feel an ache in his heart to behold it. One—and one only—resort that I know of may be this beautiful already: Zermatt.

Cars cannot reach Zermatt—the road stops some miles away and you enter by train steeply, haltingly. Without cars, the village stays white all winter—no brown slushy streets, no air blue with exhaust smoke, no noise of engines, horns, spinning tires, cursing drivers. The village is white and charming and quiet except for sleighbells and perhaps a neighing horse, and above the village rise those mountains. They are majestic, grandiose, gorgeous in all directions. To the south they are even more than this.

To the south thrusts the Matterhorn—not God's greatest mountain by any means, but surely His most stunning. With luck our skier will come up to Zermatt in a stout fog. This is what I would wish him anyway. I saw the Matterhorn first after having looked for it all day through the clouds. I had heard it was handsome and very high, and so my wife and I looked for it out of the window for hours, and later searched for it through the streets of the town. But the clouds were low and dense everywhere.

Several times the clouds parted, exposing peaks which seemed high. Each time we wondered if this peak, finally, was the celebrated Matterhorn.

After dinner we walked again, and then suddenly the clouds parted at last and there it was with the moonlight on it, incredibly high and lovely. We looked at each other but did not speak. There was no need to say: "Do you suppose that this is it?" We knew. We knew.

Our ideal resort begins to take shape. It is beautiful and no cars go in there. Cars, for me at least, soil and spoil a resort and I am always happiest where there are none: Zermatt, Wengen, Mürren, a few others. After that the ideal resort should be both very high (to permit the best possible skiing for the maximum number of months) and very low, so as to be decently warm and not cause any high-altitude headaches. Obviously this is a contradiction, but we are dealing in ideals, are we not?

The highest resort in the Alps is Sestriere, Italy, at 6,300 feet. Sestriere also has the highest hotels, two towering towers, one of them fifteen stories up, the other twelve. You can ski in Sestriere much later than at most other places and, after riding ski lifts all day, you can ride the elevator up to bed.

I get swell headaches there. But I must say the towers are intriguing.

Most of the famous resorts are at about 5,000 to 6,000 feet, including Davos, Switzerland, where I once went skiing at 14 degrees below zero.

I look back on this as an exhilarating experience, brag about it to anyone who will listen, and describe the way the wind wafted ice crystals off the snow and blew them right through my bones. I rarely remember to add that the next day I took the coward's way out, fled Davos, and have not been back since. I took the train into Austria and found Kitzbühel 3,000 feet lower and 40 degrees warmer.

Ideally, then, our resort will be both as high as Sestriere and as low as Kitzbühel, and it ought to stand on a border so that you can ski in two countries the same day. This is possible at Chamonix-Courmayeur, and also at Zermatt-Cervinia. Some 11,500 feet up, above Chamonix, an aerial cable car crosses the White Valley, a distance of three dangling miles, and you can ski down into Italy if you like.

At Zermatt you must change into several different kinds of lifts to do this, and the last of them is a kind of snow bulldozer which tows you along. The descent there is to Italy, too.

As for trails, our ideal resort should have at least a few long, long runs (Davos, Chamonix, and Zermatt all claim trails longer than ten miles) and, for the brave souls among us, at least one insanely difficult downhill track (like the Lauberhorn at Wengen, the Hahnenkamm at Kitzbühel, and the Piste Verte near Chamonix). Of course, the medical facilities in the valley below should be the best in the world.

The ideal resort should also have at least one great hotel so that our skier can observe real luxury before it vanishes entirely from the earth, and can observe also the princes and film stars who winter there. The most sumptuous hotel I know of is the Palace at St. Moritz, where nearly every aga, emperor and pretender of this century has put up at one time or another.

Once we arrived at the Palace "en famille," after having

driven over mountain passes all day. One of the children had been carsick about twelve times. We were exceedingly grubby, and tried to enter the Palace inconspicuously, but the other child went round and round in the revolving door until finally it slewed her across the lobby floor on her hands and knees. End of inconspicuousness.

A bellboy dressed like a pasha picked her up, and we were forced to step forward and claim our offspring. But no one snickered, or made us feel ill-dressed, and within a few minutes Andrea Badrutt, owner of the Palace, and his staff somehow made us comfortable, welcome. This is quite a trick.

I have my reservations about St. Moritz. It has rather too many great hotels, too much royalty and ex-royalty. This gets in the way of the skiing. But I have no reservations about the Palace, where King Farouk and I are treated equally well. The Palace is everybody's palace, and one of the last of same.

The ideal resort should have a permanent major ski meet in progress. Thus our skier would be able to watch how a good skier comes down the mountain, poles tucked under his arms, tightly crouched, making sixty miles an hour at least, as fast as if he had fallen off a building. This would eliminate once and for all any notion our skier might hold that he, too, is a cool, cool skier and clever enough to race if only he felt like it.

Our ideal ski resort should include all these things and more. But why go on? The ideal ski resort does not exist and, luckily for those of us who ski, it never will. For if it did, which of us would have the time and heart ever again to do an honest day's work?

PORTFOLIO 4

THE

PICTORIAL

MAGNIFICENCE

OF

SKIING

This is
La Vallée Blanche—
White Valley—
high above Chamonix,
in France.

The tension is at the top, the best place by far to watch a ski race.

Sometimes a camera can catch the skier's expression
as he rushes by.

When at last the signal is given, the skier
lunges out onto the mountain.

Sometimes
the skier
can see
for a moment
how far
is down.

Ski racing is alternately quiet grace, a kind
of soundless beauty . . .

and then it is frenzy, speed, nerves, fright. . . .

This is the Piste Verte—the Green Track. Each summer, the bull-dozers "perfect" it, and each winter when snow comes again, it is faster still.

1. White Valley provides the highest skiing in Europe, over 11,000 feet up, and in fall and spring both the view and the skiing are magnificent. This cableway crosses to a peak above Italy.

2. The 1962 World Slalom Championships at Chamonix were raced in a near blizzard. Conditions worsened from minute to minute, while each suffering skier (here Francois Bonlieu of France) waited his turn.

3. Charles Bozon of France, World Slalom Champion. As picture shows, he won race screaming.

4. Traudl Hecher of Austria, starting girls' slalom at Chamonix, 1962.

5. This is Adrien Duvillard at the start of the Hahnenkamm downhill at Kitzbühel, 1962. In downhill racing there is that terrifying view at the start, then the skier drops into a crouch, the wind rushes by, and he doesn't see much of anything. At 60 miles per hour at times, only reflexes and memory keep a skier from disaster.

6. Here Egon Zimmerman of Austria glides to the giant World Slalom Championships, Chamonix, 1962.

7. And here Bonlieu crashes within sight of victory, to lose the Hahnenkamm Slalom, Kitzbühel, 1962.

8. The Piste Verte—the Green Track—near Chamonix, is one of the world's fastest, and is getting faster every year.

AUTHOR'S NOTE:

Much of the text in this book appeared originally in somewhat different form in *The New York Times,* to whose editors I am grateful for permission to use it here. I first covered sports in Europe for the *Times* at the 1956 Winter Olympics at Cortina d'Ampezzo, Italy. The *Times's* sports department was in flux then. Frank Blunk was feature editor, responsible for getting one sports feature a day in the paper. He took a chance on me. An experienced man was to report the events at Cortina. But if I paid my own way to Cortina and wrote some features, Mr. Blunk would get them in the paper and I would probably finish with a profit over and above expenses. We went to Europe third class by ship. My wife and our first daughter stayed with her parents at Nice, and I went on to Cortina third class by rail, sitting up all night in a crowded compartment, worrying about money. At Cortina I was lodged in the press hotel, on condition that I guaranteed to stay till the end of the games. That is, I guaranteed the hotel $15 a day for seventeen days—$255. I was twenty-five years old, this was a lot of money to me, and I remember thinking that it was an investment in my future. But I had never made an investment before, and in my panic, I hesitated a long time before I finally signed the paper. Mr. Blunk had told me to send "four or five" features. We had plotted some of them out. But the Olympics were exciting, I sent a story every day, and no one told me to stop. Later Mr. Blunk told me I had done well. I felt incredibly proud. I owe a great deal

178

ROBERT DALEY

to that man, and if he won't be too embarrassed, I would like to say thank you, publicly, one more time.

In 1958 James Roach became sports editor of the *Times,* features were still being sought, and we were back in Europe again, though with two children now. Mr. Roach agreed to use some more pieces from me, and even added some expense money. I reported car races from Holland, Germany, France, Italy, still riding third class trying to make Jim Roach and the *Times* think I was a bargain.

The next year I was taken on more or less permanently to cover events, and to write a column called "Sports in Europe" each Tuesday. We lived in Nice, and from there, all expenses paid, I set out each weekend to the far corners of Europe: to Lisbon, Palermo, Prague, Liverpool and other places nearer and somewhat easier to get to. I was feeling my way, and on occasion turned up places to report events which didn't exist. Everybody was very kind. We didn't starve and I didn't get fired.

When I left New York, Jim Roach had said: "Get a camera. If we use any of your pictures you get a few dollars extra."

I bought a secondhand Kodak Retina, and that first weekend took about fourteen pictures of the World Bobsledding Championships at St. Moritz. Then the camera froze. I sent the film to New York, and four of those pictures were used the next Sunday. I was elated, and felt rich. I bought some more film. Later on I bought more and better cameras. My cameras freeze less now than they used to, as does the man behind them.

ROBERT DALEY
Paris, April, 1963